❧

You Alone Are Real to Me

*This book was made possible with
the generous support of
Mary S. Mulligan Charitable Trust*

Love Song

How should I hold my soul, so that it
does not touch on yours? How should I
lift it beyond you, to other things?
Oh, I would gladly shelter it amidst
lost shadows of some forgotten spot where
it might not swing when your depths stir.
But all that touches us, yes everything
brings us together like the bow-string
which pulls from two strings a single chord.
Over what instrument are we so tightly drawn?
By the hand of which violinist are we thus born?
Oh sweet song.

R.M. RILKE, *New Poems,* 1907

You Alone
Are Real to Me

REMEMBERING RAINER MARIA RILKE

by Lou Andreas-Salomé

Translated with an
Introduction and Afterword by

Angela von der Lippe

American Readers Series, No. 6

BOA Editions, Ltd. ❧ Rochester, New York ❧ 2003

Rainer Maria Rilke © Insel Verlag Frankfurt am Main 1988
English Translation © 2003 by Angela von der Lippe
Introduction and Afterword © 2003 by Anglea von der Lippe

First Edition

01 02 03 04 7 6 5 4 3 2 1

Cover design: Daphne Poulin-Stofer
Cover photos: Rainer Maria Rilke and author photo courtesy
Suhrkamp Verlag. Photo of translator by Jim Jordan.
Interior photos: Pages 75 and 76 courtesy of Suhrkamp Verlag; pages
77 and 78 courtesy of The Freud Museum Publications, London.
Interior design and composition: Valerie Brewster, Scribe Typography
BOA Logo: Mirko

LIBRARY OF CONGRESS CATALOGING-IN-PUBLICATION DATA

Andreas-Salomé, Lou, 1861–1937
[Rainer Maria Rilke. English]
You alone are real to me: remembering Rainer Maria Rilke / by Lou
Andreas-Salomé; translated, and with an introduction and afterword
by Angela von der Lippe. — 1st ed.
    p. cm. — (American reader series; no. 6)
Includes bibliographical references.
ISBN 1-929918-32-1 (alk. paper)
1. Rilke, Rainer Maria, 1875–1926. 2. Authors, Austrian — 20th century
— Biography. 1. Title. 11. Series: American reader series; v. 6.
PT2635.165Z56813 2003
831'.912 — DC21
                                                           2003043670

BOA Editions, Ltd.
Steven Huff, Publisher
H. Allen Spencer, Chair, Board of Directors
A. Poulin, Jr., President & Founder (1976–1996)
260 East Avenue, Rochester, NY 14604
www.boaeditions.org

CONTENTS

The Young Poet Meets His Muse:
An Introduction

Sometimes I want to lift myself out of this silence
and ascend to you as if to the saint of that distant
homeland that I cannot reach—[I am] so seized
with the knowledge that you are the bright star
that stands directly above the location of my
darkest and most fearful self.

RAINER MARIA RILKE IN A LETTER TO
LOU ANDREAS-SALOMÉ, AUGUST, 15, 1903

Poets have always had their muses, and Rainer Maria Rilke was no exception. But Rilke's muse was different. She was more than that dark lady of the poetic imagination who commands a netherworld of coy expectancy, defies apprehension by the senses, and ultimately inhabits the fluid shadows of genius. Much more than his creation, Rilke's muse was for him the quintessential experience of an external reality that he struggled to appropriate for himself. She was a woman and a grande dame of her age; her name was Lou Andreas-Salomé.

When one reads the biographies, the memoirs, and the correspondence between Rilke and Andreas-Salomé, there can be no question that Lou wielded a singularly powerful influence on Rilke's poetic development and that she assumed the qualities so often attributed to the poet's muse.[1] Embodying that strange mixture of dominant mother and submissive mistress, she both set a critical standard for Rilke's craftsmanship, and coaxed the passionate abandon that inspired breakthroughs in his work. Communicating throughout Rilke's adult life from great distances of intimacy, she was pursued as inspiration and hearkened to as critic and editor. Because Lou was quite real and not imagined, she stood apart from, but not necessarily in opposition to, Rilke's art;

and she could not be subsumed as the means to the self-centered end of the poet's creation. Thus, as the guardian of both his life and his art, Lou represented in a profound sense not merely the challenge for Rilke, but the reward, the very possibility of combining those seemingly incompatible aspects of his experience.

> And Lou, I believe this must be so. This is one life and that is another; and we are not made to have two lives.... For isn't it true, Lou?; it has to be so. We should be like a stream and not wander into canals and carry water into the pastures. Isn't it true, we should hold ourselves firmly together and roar? Perhaps when we are old, we will be permitted to spread ourselves out and empty into a delta.... dear Lou!
>
> Rilke to Lou, Aug. 8, 1903, Briefwechsel

The story of Rilke and Lou is not then merely the affirmation of a Faustian principle of knowledge acquired through the "eternally feminine." Their friendship is a modest declaration of a dark and erotic entanglement between two uniquely literary and modern lovers. Indeed, this muse survived the death of her beloved charge to celebrate his afterlife and to speak with grace and eloquence about her personal loss and the enduring legacy of Rilke's poetic art.

When Lou first met Rilke in the summer of 1897, she was an accomplished woman of thirty-six who had secured for herself an enviable reputation as a writer of sundry essays, the novels *Ruth* and *Searching for God*, a biography of

Friedrich Nietzsche, and varied literary criticism, including a work on Henrik Ibsen's heroines (see *Ibsen's Heroines*, translated by Siegfried Mandel [Redding Ridge, CT: Black Swan Books, 1986]). In contrast, Rilke was a fledgling poet of twenty-two from the provinces of Austria who had come to Munich to establish himself in the society that had already embraced Lou and her literary circle. They met on the evening of May 12, in the apartment of a well-known novelist, Jakob Wassermann. In a letter that Rilke sent to Lou the following day, we have the first record of an intimate correspondence that would continue in fits and spurts, but with consistent intensity, for nearly three decades, until the poet's death in 1926.

Indeed, the first words of Rilke's letter to Lou resonate with the excitement, conviction, and immediacy of a suitor seduced by the urgency of full disclosure and impelled by the desperate need to invest the elusive moment of their meeting with the enduring meaning of inevitable union. Seizing the opportunity to compliment Lou on an essay he had read on a previous winter evening, Rilke opens with the coy, presumptuous claim that yes, of course, they had met before: "Yesterday was not the first twilight hour that I was graced with your presence." He goes on to draw a parallel between Lou's essay "Jesus the Jew" and his cycle of poems entitled "Visions of Christ"—a parallel that is, as he claims, not merely of passing interest but of deep significance: "It was not just interest that led me deeper and deeper into this revelation but rather it was a believer's trust that propelled me forward until finally it was cause for jubilation when I discovered—what my dream epics render in visions was expressed here so masterfully with the gigantic force of holy conviction ... through this unshakable parsimony, through the relentless force of your words, my work became consecrated and was sanctioned in my feeling." Rilke further asserts that Lou's essay relates to his poems as does dream to reality, wish to fulfillment. And he reasons that he needs to convey his personal gratitude to her in a setting as private as that of their first meeting: "To me it seems always that when someone thanks another for something truly valuable, that gratitude should remain a secret between the two parties." He concludes by stating that his words are but long overdue thanks and that their expression represents a sign.

The realization of dream, wish fulfillment, the sanction of feelings, and conspiratorial gratitude for a grand coincidence of fate, their secret tryst. Those were the words with which Rilke merged Lou with the deepest yearnings of his identity and conferred on her the role of muse. From the moment when Rilke first jubilantly announced his presence to Lou, he assumed a posture of pursuit that would persist, albeit in modified form, throughout their thirty-year friendship. Rilke was not only the one to initiate the friendship, he was invariably the one to reestablish contact after long lapses in communication. Although not all the correspondence between Rilke and Lou has been preserved (an estimated one tenth of Rilke's letters [13] and one-third of Lou's letters [35] have been lost), it can be inferred from references within the letters that Rilke clearly wrote more often and at greater length, and much more in the mode of a correspondent soliciting a response, than did Lou (see *Briefwechsel*, p. 622). Indeed, Rilke's first letters, abundant in hyperbole and written in the passionate throes of a lover's self-discovery, suggest the almost medieval stance of a minnesinger toward his noble lady. Lou was idealized, and Rilke stood there, his "heart burning before her mercy, like a lamp before the image of Mary...." (Rilke to Lou, June 9, 1897). He declared his servitude and likened himself to the "scepter of the queen — only I do not make you rich. I am yours, just as the last tiny star belongs to the night, that hardly knows it and does not recognize its light...." (Rilke to Lou June 8, 1897)

And yet, as a consequence of his unqualified adoration, Rilke suffered the full frustration of their unequal relationship. Entries from Rilke's *Florentine Diary*, which began in the form of a letter to Lou, illustrate well the enormity of this painful imbalance. Lou's undocumented but presumed critical reception of Rilke's poetic celebration of love only exacerbated his sense of intellectual inferiority and he wrote:

> I hated you as something too great. I wanted for once to be the wealthy one, the one bearing gifts, the master, and you were the one who should come to me and accept the warm hospitality of my care and my love. And once again I was the smallest beggar on the last threshold of your presence that stood on such broad and secure pillars....

p. 34

7

In another entry from the diary Rilke alludes to the discrepancy between his and Lou's comparative experience, if not specifically to their age difference: "My struggles are your long-won victories and for this reason I stand so small before you. But my new victories belong to you, and these are what I am permitted to give you...." (p. 35)

But Lou and Rilke were not medieval lovers, and they were not completely constrained by the sexual mores of their time. When they met, Lou had been married for ten years to a translator of Persian and specialist in Oriental languages, Friedrich Carl Andreas, who was fifteen years her senior. It was a marriage of peculiar convenience that Lou had finally consented to in order to save Andreas from his self-destructive urges. (In Lou's presence, Andreas had once threatened to kill himself, plunging a knife into his chest.) Before her marriage, Lou had been the object of many a man's amorous intentions: the pastor Hendrik Gillot, who had nurtured her intellectual awakening in adolescence; the doctor-philosopher Paul Reé, with whom she lived for three years; and the philosopher Friedrich Nietzsche, with whom she had hoped to share her home with Reé in a pious and fecund "trinity" of intellectual study and sexual abstinence. Given Lou's open defiance of convention and the sexual restraint that characterized early liaisons, it is difficult not to see her marriage to Andreas as logically consistent with the pursuit of her intellectual ambitions in a sexually neutralized context.

It is true that during the years immediately following her marriage to Andreas, Lou's resolve regarding sexual abstinence was tested in a relationship with the journalist and social activist Georg Ledebour; in the end, however, Lou rejected Ledebour's overtures and returned to the curious refuge of her marriage. It comes then as a particularly unexpected surprise to discover that in 1897 this older worldly-wise woman would take the young poet and suitor as her first lover. Whether this signaled for Lou the submission to erotic impulses, the conscious—and safe—decision to give herself to a much younger, dependent man, or simply a personal maturation process, is the stuff of which literary gossip is made. It was surely all those things, but most simply it was a break from Lou's former resolve—a first event that, like all firsts, acquires exaggerated proportions but which, in this case, resonates with the significance Lou and Rilke gave to each other first as lovers and later as friends. Lou and Rilke's friendship was as dramatically compelling in its development as it had been unexpected in its beginnings. Theirs was a union that survived the early pain of sexual acceptance and rejection to mature into a dialogue that sustained them both throughout their lifetimes. And this continued dialogue alone attests to a certain transcendent quality in their love that allowed them both to acknowledge their personal limitations without relinquishing the depth of feeling that they had shared for each other.

During the first passionate years of their love affair, Rilke was a frequent guest at Lou's house and they traveled twice to Lou's homeland of Russia—first in the company of Andreas and later alone together. During that early period Lou grew into the role of mentor and introduced Rilke to a culture that he embraced however naively as "a gift of the primal childhood he had been deprived of." Russia gave Rilke a sense of community without boundaries and a belief in a deity that inhabited the earth and expressed its divinity in human potential. Indeed, Russia and Lou (to the extent that she had been cause for Rilke's acquaintance with Russia and could call Russia her true homeland) had made an indelible and critical impression on Rilke's artistic sensibility. As if a fundamental alienation had been transcended, Rilke abandoned the stylized forms of his early poems (*The Book of Pictures*) for a more open and deeply personal verse (*The Book of Hours*). This Russian God mediated through Lou was divested of its historical remove and the mystical trappings of liturgy; instead this God manifested Himself in earthly creation, an immanent reality that the poet through his words could reclaim as his own. Rilke's poetic tongue was unleashed and he declared that he had found in Lou "a new ground for loneliness and a high hindrance for the other.... that Russia is my home belongs to those grand and secret certainties from which I derive life, but my attempts to go there through travel, through books, through people are more like a divergence or turning away than an approach...." (Rilke to Lou, August 15, 1903)

It would seem that Lou represented for Rilke a coincidence of sexual, aesthetic, and religious desires in a unique form that rendered these otherwise exclusive interests compatible with one another, however tentative that unity might have been felt. She encouraged the exploration of these interests and made them tangible and real. Indeed, Lou's very presence provided a locus for their cultivation outside of the self in the beloved Other. Small wonder then that Rilke would come to depend on Lou throughout his lifetime for the strength and consolation to carry him through the crises of self-doubt and over the painful thresholds into new realms of exploration in his poetry. From the sculpted object-poems of his Rodin period (*New Poems*) to the newly subjective inner landscape and the "heartwork" of the prewar period to the decade-long silence and final outcry of the *Duino Elegies*, each boundary crossed required that Rilke shed a layer of protective covering, the skin that, as Lou notes in her memoir, hemmed Rilke into himself. And each new period precipitated a crisis in identity and prompted an appeal to Lou simply to listen and to fathom the experience he could not himself comprehend.

"Lou, I — your lost prodigal son — am no storyteller, no soothsayer of my prescribed path... what you hear is only the sound of my footstep that trods along on undetermined pathways and what it leaves and whom it approaches, I do not know. Only that my mouth when it becomes a great stream will merge into you, into your listening and into the great quietude of your open depths — this is my prayer that I repeat every hour.... If my life's story is so small and insignificant... it will first exist for me when I can tell it to you and you will listen...." (Rilke to Lou, Nov. 9, 1903) Here Rilke echoes the sentiments of an earlier letter (Rilke to Lou, Aug. 8, 1903) in which he alludes to the incompatibility of art and life; once again he identifies the possibility of their union in the person of Lou. In the image of the peaceful, silent delta into which his words finally empty, he assigns to Lou the raison d'être of his poetry.

Lou continued to be the person to whom Rilke turned for enlightenment, far beyond the years of their love affair, into years of separation that witnessed Rilke's marriage to the sculptor Clara Westhoff and Lou's romantic involvement with several men. Lou became for Rilke an interpreter of his experience, but more than the wisdom she shed on any particular event it was her being, the fact of her caring, that was essential and indispensable to Rilke. In that regard, it is interesting to note that, early on, Rilke had dismissed psychoanalysis as a palliative for his inner turmoil because he feared that it was a disinfectant of the soul and could dispel (or exorcise) the angels as well as the demons. Lou's stated reluctance to prescribe such a path for her troubled friend amounted to a tacit agreement with Rilke.

The extent of Rilke's real reliance on Lou for understanding is perhaps most dramatically underscored in the record of the last days of his life. Refusing to hear the doctor's prognosis, Rilke instructed Frau Wunderly-Volkart, the attendant at his deathbed, to entrust "the whole truth" to Lou. Later, although he refused the invitation to write to Lou, Rilke nevertheless expressed several times the wan hope that maybe Lou would be able to understand the source of his illness. Stricken with acute leukemia, Rilke did not meet with Lou again, and the poet was deprived of an answer from his muse. Just as he had depended on Lou for insight into life's traumas, Rilke turned to her for understanding in death. And Lou, his survivor, assumed the task of formulating an answer for herself and for posterity in an elegant memorial to Rilke's life, the memoir that follows.

The correspondence between Rilke and Lou is testimony to his lifelong devotion to her. And in the crushing weight of this evidence of Rilke's need to be understood by Lou, it is natural to ask how much she actually did understand. What did Rilke mean to Lou, and what did she derive from their friendship? Although it certainly does not provide an unbiased and fully satisfactory answer to those questions, Lou's memoir does reveal a few clues to this mystery. At the very least it unveils an extraordinarily unique portrait of Rilke as seen through Lou's eyes.

Lou wrote her memoir of Rilke in 1927, a year after the poet died. To be sure, a retrospective view of life is cast in broad strokes and its vantage point differs radically from the small corners of the correspondence that collect the minutiae of an everyday exchange. The memoir tries to make sense of a life that is past, complete, and whole, while the letters respond to single moments of lives predicated on continuation, fragmentation, and change. Still the full significance of the memoir can only be appreciated in the context of the letters from which the memoir draws so liberally. And the comparison of these two records, the one a private memorial to life and the other a public memorial to death, allows us to approximate more accurately what really happened and to begin to plumb the depths of Lou's feeling for Rilke.

Lou opens her memoir with the seemingly paradoxical

statement that death affords us a moment of heightened awareness and an opportunity to experience for the first time the departed one's essence in the advice speaking from the silence. She goes on to discuss the inextricable unity of life and death in Rilke's poetry and to relate this aesthetic equation of life and death to Rilke's childhood experience of the death of his uncle. On that occasion death had acquired for Rilke its indelible meaning as the superabundance of life and as liberation from the menacing shackles of the body (the survivor's experience of mortality). It is an oddly philosophical and dispassionate beginning to a memoir of one's lover, but it is clear that Lou wishes to identify death as a familiar and central preoccupation—if not the wellspring—of Rilke's poetry. It is equally apparent that Lou's exclusive focus on the theme of the transcendence of death has as much specific meaning for Lou in the face of her own loss as it has general relevance for Rilke's poetry. We hear nothing in these opening pages of the inconsolable pain of her grief but rather of the irresistible attraction to genius and the enduring aching need to understand that bond.

Lou embarks on her remembrance of Rilke with an air of intellectual detachment. She speaks in a calm voice completely in concert with the cool and analytical tone that she so frequently assumed in her letters to Rilke. In those letters she had constantly sought to mute Rilke's pain as she pointed to the physiological basis of his anxiety and counseled him to externalize and contain his fear in his poetry. So, too, the memoir discusses at length and in some obsessive detail the emotional and physical manifestations of Rilke's illnesses. Yet in the flush of the letters' living dialogue Lou seems to respond as an ever-attentive mother, while in the memoir's recollection of the silenced voice of her partner she speaks with the authority and neutrality of a classical analyst. It is a curious and telling transformation that , as we can only suppose, bore distinct advantages for Lou. For the calm remove and emotional equilibrium by which Lou, in an almost maternal way, had protected Rilke against life's numerous intimations of mortality now served in the memoir the ironic purpose of protecting Lou from life's ultimate threat—the moment of death—and of preserving the illusion of Rilke's life.

If Lou's insistence in her letters on emotional control seems appropriate in the face of Rilke's dependency and his solicitations of love to which she chose not to respond, that same self-censoring caution is a disturbing fact of her memoir. Moreover, it frustrates any inquiry into the emotional bond that Lou felt for Rilke. The correspondence does, however, provide some insight into the complexity of this problem: in those moments when Lou allowed herself a direct response to Rilke. These moments are quite remarkable for their specific reference to Rilke's poetry, to the self he had re-created in his art. In these passages Lou celebrates Rilke's power to give expression to formlessness and to create the primal relatedness of human beings to one another. It would seem then that Lou saw in Rilke's poetic powers the only acceptable formulation of their union. In one such stunning and revealing passage, Lou acknowledges Rilke's writing as the medium for the expression of their union and yet she admits her own impotence to respond: "When I read your letter and the notebook entry and everything that suddenly gives expression to that which remains formless and dumb in the communings of people—then you are with me ... Yes, then you are mine. I see you again, and I truly am confident that you can undertake that strange journey that will lead you to me and to my innermost apprehension of life itself. But how should I for my part convey this same indescribable closeness ..." (Lou to Rilke, Jan. 13, 1913)

The expression of intimacy is precisely the dilemma that emerges in comparing Lou's letters with her memoir. How could she reciprocate the fullness of feeling that she scrupulously chose only to acknowledge in Rilke's poetry? As the letters attest, she could not. In fact, at least in writing, she resisted Rilke's overtures as she would so often counter his flights of romantic fantasy with the equivalent of a diminutive "Oh, Rainer." It is also worth noting that Lou, on occasion, edited out passionate exclamations in Rilke's letters—words or phrases that appealed for a direct relation to Lou unmediated by Rilke's art (e.g. Rilke to Lou, Oct. 23, 1909 and Feast of the Epiphany, 1913). But Lou did not totally rebuff her suitor. While she could not grant Rilke exclusive claim to her affections, she did seize upon the opportunity to instruct him in the saving grace of his art. Doing so was not a completely selfless act on Lou's part, for the letters attest to the progressive delight she took in his poetry. And it is not idle speculation to suggest that Rilke's work provided Lou as well with a safe haven from the passions that she had so often outlined in her own fictional work as destructive and that threatened to consume her. Lou's memoir thus documents the cultivation of an aesthetic education from a dual perspective—that of the emerging artist and, to a lesser but still palpable degree, that of Lou herself as teacher and critic.

Consistent with Lou's wish to regard Rilke as an artist, the memoir focuses exclusively on the poet; and Lou's voice bears the vestiges of formality and ritual befitting of eulogy. Lou herself is conspicuously absent from the memoir. She exists only in Rilke's direct appeals to her in excerpts from the letters. There are few references to herself—an occasional acknowledgment that she and Rilke traveled together or met on a particular occasion, but never the intrusive reflection that would betray a shared experience. An ambivalent feeling. Or is it perhaps a fairer assessment to say that Lou did not wish to bask in reflected glory? Whatever the reason may have been for her self-censorship, Lou's approach seemed to revive the familiar roles and to extend the natural dialogue in which Rilke petitions Lou for answers and she responds in understanding and analysis. In such a light the memoir may be viewed as a valiant attempt on Lou's part to suspend death's silence, if but for a brief time, and to give voice to her beloved as only he had spoken to her.

In its singular focus on Rilke the artist, Lou's memoir is quite notably sparse in its mention of other people in Rilke's life. Lou and Rilke's correspondence, as well as Rilke's correspondences with others, abound in their references to Rilke's many friends, patrons, and acquaintances. Yet the memoir itself names only a distinguished and influential few —Leo Tolstoy, Paul Valéry, and Auguste Rodin, for example —and regards them as they illuminate Rilke's artistic growth. The themes of family and domesticity; the trials of earning a living; religious feeling and health and travel are evaluated through the single lens of artistic purpose. As such, the sacrifices Rilke suffered in order to fulfill his calling are magnified and ennobled for their influence on his artistic productivity.

In a retrospective of Rilke's magnificent poetic legacy, one would be hard pressed not to assign an aesthetic value to Rilke's life struggles and his suffering. But at the same time it is only wise to recognize that such a circumscribed view of Rilke as poet tends to create the illusion of an impenetrable artistic isolation that underplays the need that Rilke so often expressed for human companionship, which he did in fact pursue. Consequently, the sense of compatibility of the aesthetic and erotic instincts is diminished and, as has already been noted in the discussion of the correspondence, this unity of art and life was most dramatically articulated in Rilke's invocation of Lou's presence. The unspoken assumption of the memoir perhaps. Hence the self-censorship exercised in the memoir extends beyond mere propriety and, oddly enough, commends to secrecy the full range of the voice that issues from the silence.

If the memoir is somewhat flawed by Lou's guarded approach toward disclosing details of the shared intimacy in their lives, it more than compensates for such deficiency through its sweeping personal insights into Rilke's development as a poet. As an immediate retrospective of his life's work, the memoir is a unique historical piece of literary criticism, remarkable intellectually in both its conception and aspirations. Lou seeks to integrate the maturation of Rilke's poetry into the metamorphosis of his awareness of self in relation to the world. That is a highly ambitious program for the literary critic—one that too often indulges in lofty aesthetic claims for the work itself or plunges into fictive reconstruction of the motivations of its creator. It presumes an access to, and understanding of, the emotional world of the poet that is ordinarily not available to the critic who, being literary, must decode and interpret a written legacy—all too often without any sense (appreciation) of the tone, the pitch, the cadence of the voice that, except for the fact of its mortality, might otherwise have been content to just speak its words. But Lou did have such access, and as we have seen in Rilke's appeals to her in their correspondence, Lou represented the critical point of intersection, the hope and frustration of lines that merged and diverged in the constant dialogue of art and life. Small wonder then that she would be privy to the moments of personal crisis that gave way to breakthroughs in Rilke's verse. As such, the memoir offers an extraordinary odyssey through the doubts, foibles, and insecurities of the poet in his quest for self-expression.

The memoir bears witness to the anxiety of silent anticipation, the ecstasy of creation, and the utter dejection of having transcended one's limits only to find oneself dumped back to earth and expelled as mere residue of the creative process. Perhaps more than any other source, the memoir gives its readers glimpses of the emotional adjustments that accompanied each new phase of discovery in Rilke's poetry —the struggle of the poet to redefine the parameters of his power according to the new perspective that the work at hand afforded him. Hence the grand transports: from the submission to the unrequited yet all-embracing love of the "neighboring" God of *The Book of Hours*, through the physical displacement of a fabricated external reality in the "object-poems" of the *New Poems* and the translations, to the complete spiritual alienation in the otherworldliness of the angels in the *Duino Elegies*. Of course, there is a mediating overlay to Lou's analysis that views those transformations as a progressive confrontation of the spirit with bodily existence, Rilke's own mortality. What Lou suggests is the gradual leave-taking of the poet from his own creation, its impressions, its palpable visible reality, and, finally, spiritual inspiration itself.

The poet is engaged in a life-and-death struggle to overcome "the body's abuse of the soul" and to realize the "peace of the animals and the safety of the angels." The body deprived of consciousness, consciousness deprived of the body. In the face of the ever-widening gap between physical reality and psychic existence, the poet conjures up the saving grace of an image—the angel. Nowhere is Lou's analysis quite as penetrating as in her discussion of the significance of Rilke's pursuit of the angel.

The angel has always been a richly evocative image for Rilke, but it first achieved heroic proportions as a central figure in the *Duino Elegies*. The ten elegies of this cycle were in themselves a monumental work generated over a ten-year period. The first two elegies were written under the patronage of Princess Marie Thurn-und-Taxis-Hohenloe[2] at Schloss Duino on the Adriatic Sea in 1912; during the subsequent two years two others were written in fits and spurts, only to be followed by a lengthy silence that was finally broken in February of 1922 when Rilke composed the six remaining elegies within the solitude of his chosen hermitage, the Château de Muzot in Switzerland.

In her memoir Lou characteristically does not bother with the extraordinary facts of the elegies' production; rather, she focuses on the heroic aspect of the elegies themselves—the creation of the angel—for the angel represents the transcendent reality that affirmed Rilke's quest to unite life and death in his art. In a letter to his Polish translator Hulewicz, Rilke hinted at the tragic admission of mortality implicit in his celebration of the angel's existence: "The angel of the *Elegies* is the Being who sees in the Invisible a higher order of reality: terrible, therefore for us, because, we, who love and are transformed by him, still cling to the visible." (See *The Sacred Threshold*, p. 154.)

As the angel illuminates the beauty of artistic creation that exists independently of the mediator of its expression, the angel as no other symbol of artistic striving calls into question the being of its creator, the poet himself. In the midst of that schism, the poet must labor selflessly to interest these mediating images of the "deux inversus"—the god who is turning away and does not allow redemption—in the things of his own world. The poet's realization of the utter separateness of the realm of the angels exposes the brilliant summit of creative truth that is revealed only within the shadows of the abyss. Yet Lou maintains that such an extreme and terrifying vision of a completely polarized creator and creation did not consign Rilke to a self-denying despair; rather, it informed his struggle for self-avowal. Hence a theme of renewal permeates the elegies and culminates in Rilke's triumphant imperative to celebrate earthly existence in the opening lines of the "Ninth Elegy":

> Praise the world to the angel, not the unsayable,
> you can't impress him with grand emotion: in
>   the cosmos,
> where he feels so much more, you are a novice ...

Lou sees in Rilke's extraordinary confrontation with the stronger presence of the angel a dual recognition of the infinite resources of spiritual transcendence in art and the eclipsed reality of the artist's own mortality. For Rilke, that recognition was a mature insight free of the earlier indulgence of romantic illusions of merging God with his own creation in *The Book of Hours* or himself with creation in the objects of the *New Poems*. And it signaled both the acceptance of art's exclusive claims as well as a resignation to the limitations of his own body. Lou fixates on that duality and draws parallels to Rilke's earliest childhood fears of mortality and his later persistent anxieties about life-threatening illnesses. But she sees in the *Elegies* the sole means of transcending that dichotomy in a triumphant affirmation of self in life as well as in death: in Rilke's discovery of the angel.

Early in her memoir Lou includes a quote from one of Rilke's letters that art is the "dark wish of all things" that seek to become the images of our secrets. Rilke goes on to bemoan the poet's impotent failure to fathom the deeper connections that united him to his art, the wish to its image, because, she surmised, they were too similar. It is difficult to read these lines and not to hear those haunting questions that echo from the "Ninth Elegy":

> Earth, is it not this that you want: invisibly
> to resurrect in us? Isn't it your dream,
> to be invisible one day? — Earth, Invisible!
> What if not transformation, is your urgent mission?

There follows the poet's commitment to his art, which comes in the form of a declaration of love:

> Earth, beloved. I will.

Is this the eroticism that Lou found so appealing and comforting in Rilke's later verse? Are the *Elegies* perhaps the delta into which her beloved suitor's passion for life and art were finally allowed to merge and empty? These are the unspoken questions posed by the memoir. Alas, the muse has no answer, but true to her calling, she directs our search for the man to the surviving voice of his poems—"the advice that arises from silence."

Several years after Lou had written her memoir, she wrote a brief remembrance of Rilke in which she recalled his spirit and spoke to him as she presumably had wanted to do in his presence:

> If for years I was your woman, it was because you were for me the first real truth—indistinguishable body and human spirit, undeniable proof of life itself. Word for word, I could have repeated to you what you said to me as a confession of love: "You alone are real to me." With these words we were wed, before we had even become friends. And we became friends hardly by choice but rather through a subliminally consummated marriage. Two halves did not seek completion in each other. But a surprised whole recognized itself in an unfathomable totality. So then we were rather like primal siblings, before incest had become sacrilege.

Lebensrückblick, p. 139

Rainer Maria Rilke

By Lou Andreas-Salomé

Mourning is not as singular a state of emotional preoc-cupation as is commonly thought: it is, more precisely, an incessant discourse with the departed one, in order to draw him nearer. For death entails not merely a disappearance but rather a transformation into a new realm of visibility. Something is not just taken away but is gained, in a way never before experienced. In the moment when the flowing lines of a figure's constant change and effect become paralyzed for us, we are imbued for the first time with its essence: something which is never captured or fully realized in the normal course of lived existence.

This new process transpires with the same involuntary immediacy as that of previous personal exchanges; it does not result from the intentional solace or celebration of the willful yearnings of thought. Indeed, not even the impressions or intervening motives of the past can disrupt the passionate possession of this experience that affords us access to what had been previously inconceivable: in waiting for the news that issues from the silent one—Listen to the stirrings! That uninterrupted advice that arises from tranquillity.

This is how it was for me around the turn of the year 1926/27, that "blustering threatening one," as Rainer Maria Rilke described it in a letter from his deathbed. The perplexing distinction between survival and death had become so small. Indeed, we were overwhelmed with the realization that all social intercourse ends in the violence of our own submission. And are not the most cherished ones, in particular, but signs and images of our earliest submissions to love, from which we first learned to love, perhaps even before they (the cherished ones) lived—so like the easterly cloud formation that is illuminated by the sun setting in the western sky? And during our lifetime we know so little of that brilliance to which we are so thoroughly bound that it can never be extinguished. There is the loved one who remains in a coffin, perhaps more lamentable in death than any; and there is that other beloved who wishes to make his presence known to us and who answers us in a lively dialogue that becomes itself an ever-changing reality because it touches on that which unites us eternally with life and death.

When one considers what Rilke had produced by the mid-nineties—"An Offering to the Lares," "Crowned with Dreams," poems from his self-edited "Wegwarten" (Wild Chicory) notebooks, as well as a few novellas no longer preserved—one cannot escape the impression of a seminal interdependence between the poet and death. The nearness of death reflected in the objects the poet celebrates in verse—their life permeating things that are fragile, ephemeral, and vulnerable—inspires his poetic vision. In dying these things exhale a beauty that is their share of eternity, and, accordingly, the tone in which they speak to us is a quiet, overwhelmingly gentle one, now and then plucking the strings of sentimentality. But this has given rise to a common misunderstanding that has consigned Rilkean poetry to a false romanticism; for from the beginning Rilke sang of mortal beings, not of death but of life. Poetry was that reality which embraced both. And only because the hideously healthy ones refuse to have anything to do with death did he choose to commune with those who walked the boundary on which the poor inaccessible words of life and death are exchanged. It was never the ambition of this poet, so born to the poetry of life, to flatter death in verse; he wanted nothing more than somehow to express reality as he saw it, be it sometimes starkly cruel and devoid of tenderness. Poetry could be nothing but his experience of reality compressed into words that were voiced as oaths—essence, not sound. For as much a paradox as this may seem, I would go so far as to claim that this poet of the supra-sensual was in fact robust. Somehow from the beginning he was destined to prove with short attack that, biblically spoken, the heavenly realm of the Almighty belongs to those who do not at first expect it, but rather have mastered it, and who know one urgent, inviolable, and imperturbable necessity—the unity of life and death. This almost indescribable quality of being unchanging and free of the noticeable yearnings of development—this presence and sense of visible immanence—lent him the peculiar charm of arrested youth.

It explains why even at the onset of his twenties he had no long-range goals in life, no impatient hunger for the experience that might await him in the "red violence which so many call life," as he noted in one of his earliest letters. Just not to let what had been entrusted to him in safety and determination be torn asunder. Without fearing for himself he preferred to retreat with it under one roof. He was like one who carefully and respectfully holds a priceless vessel in both hands and avoids what might disturb it and knock it over; for anything from outside could cause that to happen without his doing. He is externally exposed and unsafe. More precisely, he is vulnerable in his corporeality, in the fact that his outermost exterior ultimately hems him into himself, clings to him and cannot be suspended in internal experience. There is no doubt that he was plagued by fears about his physical well-being; "I will soon succumb—be it my heart or lungs...." was one of his earliest statements to me, although then and throughout his life there was no reason to question his health. But when asked about it, he often spoke as if his suspicions had some basis in past experience. These lay before experience, as if buried in a dim past that defied recollection yet impressed itself on all his remembrances. It was as if he had been born into a world as though pushed before a half-hostile audience; hence, his insecurities toward his own body, that region where the external and the internal were thrust together and had to agree to appear as one and the same. The fact that his mother had tried to transform him into little Renee, a substitute for the daughter who had died before his birth, can only have contributed to those insecurities.

In his childhood his feelings seemed to have wavered between his parents, who in discord and separation pushed the little boy back and forth between them. Eventually his father gained the advantage but to no good, when he entrusted his son's education to the military school in St. Pölten. This period encompassed for Rilke's entire life his most frightening memories. Barely grown, he ran away from school, but not without some bitterly adventurous consequences. At home he was finally allowed to complete his *Abitur* (diploma). For this he was indebted to his uncle, who provided him with the means to obtain the necessary private tutoring. As far as I know, it seems that his uncle exerted the only positive influence on the boy; he gained his uncle's trust, and the boy's steadfastness succeeded in dispelling all doubt about his perseverance. The child actively sought to become an equally responsible man—albeit not as a lawyer but as a country doctor. Indeed he embraced his uncle's death with a peculiar reverence. Apparently, this strong and healthy man died of a stroke; but to Rilke he had appeared to be such a pillar of strength that it was as if his uncle had simply expended his health in order to make room for death at the appropriate moment—which appeared to happen as if he had burst from his own superabundance of blood. For the first time, there emerges from a childhood fantasy the notion of "one's own death," which was to gain such great significance in *The Notebooks of Malte Laurids Brigge*. Death, the just one, as proof of life, as confirmation of the self; death, as only an ancillary gesture in the pantomime of life; the progression not merely toward ruination but toward expression. Thus the meaning of death must be capable of transformation into its opposite, into the freedom from that which is menacing in bodily experience and suffering, until the common terms really do stand for each other. In *The Book of Hours* there is a poem dedicated to "the voice of a young brother"; to some degree it betrays the youthful self of the poet:

> I am running out, I am running out
> like sand slipping through my fingers.
> All at once I have so many senses
> that each thirsts so differently.
> I feel myself swell with pain
> in a hundred places.
> But mostly within my heart.
> I want to die. Leave me alone.
> I think I will succeed
> in so frightening myself
> that my pulse will burst.

Another poem that presages later ones contains the same dual conception of death as a symbol of the actual life to which it refers:

> I stand as if blind and in total darkness
> because my look no longer finds its way to you.
> The mad rush of days is
> only a curtain, behind which you exist.
> I stare up to see if it is not lifted,
> the curtain behind which my life lives.
> My life's strength, my life's necessity
> and yet: my death.

Where that which is out of the ordinary is driven to take form in life, it hardly requires the specific instances of disillusionment to break the illusion; for this the limitations of human existence itself suffice for life to fail in the face of its great internal demands. The average human destiny advances toward gradual conformity. But with genius it comes to a questioning of life itself, be it that later on some basic event is made responsible for this, be it that it dresses judgement in some conclusive image, whereby the felt tension is no longer allowed to be resolved simply and harmlessly. For Rilke there was a kind of image, a symbol in which an inborn life declared itself as a given fate; this perhaps elucidates one of his earliest childhood dreams that recurred from time to time. He dreamt that he lay near an open grave, before a tall gravestone that threatened to topple into the grave at the slightest movement. His anxiety was actually provoked by his name that he saw engraved on the precipitous stone, so that it could be mistaken for him, if it disappeared forever into the grave beneath him. This image came back to haunt him in nightmares and in feverish semiconscious states that he once described in a letter from Paris (the end of June, 1903):

> Long ago in my childhood, in the great fevers of its illnesses, huge indescribable fears arose, fears of something too large, too hard, too close, deep unspeakable fears that I remember....

The way he spoke of bodily states, of odd occurrences and anxieties, reminded him in some way of this dream; it summoned up the brutal challenges to unite under one guise two antithetical postures—those of being erect and being downtrodden: eternal annihilation in the smothering softness of the earth's bed and the transcendence of stone as a landmark and memorial to the invincible. One sometimes encounters similar dreamt anxieties, that mixture of suffering and violence, in pubescent boys before they have fully acknowledged their sexual identity and recognized their bodily needs as their own. But even if this confusing feeling of bisexuality persists for a long time afterwards, it is overcome by physical maturity; it is corrected through the opposite sex. The erotic partnership brings the blessing of clear unequivocal identity. This is not always the case with a person with burgeoning creative abilities. Natural physical maturity spawns a dangerous rivalry; in differing degrees its powers are claimed by the workplace and not by a real partnership. Inclined toward compromise, there results a greater paralysis in the corporeal processes; the unwilling attention directed to these things gives rise to proclamations of disgust that are repressed longings for pleasure. They cloak the body in melancholy and elicit a hypochodriacal oversensitivity. This danger does not decrease, as is commonly the case, but rather can escalate as the maturing person realizes his productive potential in the actual work of art; that is to say, living as a parasite on personal well-being, behaving in a vampire-like manner toward that which is most directly consummated in sexual union. For Rilke his body became more and more the pillar of suffering, the source of doubt, although he himself possessed not the slightest trace of ascetic inclinations but rather that full enjoyment of the senses, the sensual, that is indispensable to the artist. ("To transform joy is the object of all art...."—letter of November 23, 1905.) But the body's inability to partake of the joy of creating distressed him the longer, the more it kept him from achieving the clarity and wholeness that he so desired. The impertinent renunciation that he initially experienced as something external to himself was transformed over the course of time into a mistrust of himself. Each productive phase took its toll in the fatigue and illnesses that plagued him during the intervening periods when he should have been allowed to regain his strength. For this reason he later looks back longingly on the beautiful and "irretrievable" years of his youth.

> Oh how in my youth, in the face of all that need, I
> was for the most part unrecognizable, but then again
> totally accepted and taken to heart. For this reason,
> so difficult to discard and yet so quizzically hard to
> cure. Oh how the simplest pleasure that occurred to
> me could at the same time encircle the most secret
> soul. When I felt the morning air, it went through me
> so that the morning's lightness and advent permeated
> all the gradations of my nature; if I tasted a fruit, it
> rose on my tongue like a word of the spirit that van-
> ishes—the experience of that which remains inde-
> structible. Its pure enjoyment arose in all the visible
> and invisible vessels of my being.

June, 1914, from Paris

And so in this way he depicts the openness and hopefulness

of 1897 in Munich where he had lived for years, as well as the summer at Wolfratshaus before he moved to Schmargendorf in Berlin. While still in Munich he wrote:

> I question myself so often these days, as always in a time of great change. I am in the first dawn of a new epoch. — I am expelled from the garden in which I have tarried and grown weary so long.

Recalling that time he once wrote (1903, from Rome):

> The world lost its cloudiness for me, that fluid formation and dissolution that was the style and grace of my early verse; things were formed — animals that were distinguishable, flowers that really existed. Slowly, with difficulty, I learned the simple truth of how simple everything is. And I matured enough to speak of simple things.

To be "mature enough to speak of simple things" was even then his one goal, to resist the indulgence of rapture as something insufficient and groping, even if it crushed him artistically. One of his earliest letters from Munich in which he included some poems expresses it aptly:

> My confession is becoming more simple and modest — 'til that time when I will speak to you quite simply and you will simply understand.

> June, 9, 1897

No doubt his labor with Russian poetry was connected with his desire to make more comprehensible to me his poetic confession of life. Russian language and literature remained uppermost in his interests during those years, although his plans for university study never materialized despite the personal interest that Georg Simmel took in his work. In just a few clear days the *Cornet* (*Die Weise von Liebe and Tod des Cornets Christoph Rilke*) was conceived, which would later become so famous and which its author found so amazing: "… the shy ensign let go a cry like a sergeant." The poetry volumes *Advent, In Celebration of Myself* (*Advent, Mir zur Feier*), and, finally, the best achievement of all, *The Book of Pictures* (*Das Buch der Bilder*) were compiled; at the same time the *Stories of the Beloved God* (*Geschichten vom lieben Gott*) were told. This prose work is reminiscent of the chatty, affected tone of the earlier unpreserved novellas and as such is quite inferior to the poems. The *Stories* are characterized by a predominantly Russian subject matter. Before Easter 1899, Rilke took a long-planned trip to Moscow where we all (three of us, including my husband, Friedrich Carl Andreas), visited the old man, Leo Tolstoy, whom we (Rilke and I) were to visit again the following year at Yasnaya Poliana. Although Tolstoy had vehemently warned us against participating in the superstitious customs of the peasants, that Easter evening following our visit we found ourselves under the powerful influence of the Kremlin bells. Rilke refers to this celebration in a letter from Rome in 1904:

> Only once have I truly experienced Easter: it was that long, unusual, strange, exciting night when all the people pressed upon us and Iwan Welikii (the famous

bell) pounded at me blow for blow in the darkness. That was my Easter and I think it will suffice for the rest of my life. The message was delivered to me that evening in such a strangely grand way—given to me in blood and in the heart.

Later in the early summer of 1900 after the second journey of several months to Russia, if he reflects at all on the meaning of that country as a redemption for him, he does so most profoundly in *The Book of Hours*. For it was conceived there from the most immediate experience of the hours, verse for verse, prayer for prayer, suspended through days and nights that were filled with inexhaustible devotion—as perhaps has never before been revealed in poetry or prayer. It was as if both only needed to "be" because they were one and the same. This is found in the name of God that cloaks everything in *The Book of Hours* like a mantle of motherhood under which, and through which, even the most insignificant thing is baptized in its own name. This Russian God does not reign as a strange abstract authority; no, not in this way does he gain credence in the hearts of those who fear life. He can not prevent or improve all things; he can only represent closeness and intimacy for all time (in the manner of Ljeskow's [the Russian religious poet] beautiful image of him residing under the left shoulder, near the heart of man). This all-pervasive sense of security, this omnipresence, leads to a confidence in the surroundings, whatever they may be, and it presupposes an untorn integration with one's childhood, within the unity of the womb. It was exactly that childlike purity and the primitiveness in basic outlook on life (so characteristic of the Russian spirit) that captured the imagination of the poet and was released in his language. It made possible the return to a kind of familiar divinity in mankind, as if Rilke were suddenly presented with the gift of the primal home and childhood he had been deprived of. Here he confronted himself as a child in the same way that a child's conception of God emerges from the experiences of the parental home. In keeping with the prescribed conditions that here God was not necessarily synonymous with omnipotence, the prayers of *The Book of Hours* are not the product of a changed existence that has been finally realized. Now, just as before, the depression of wrenching and desperate hours could be felt between the stanzas. Only the attitude toward such periods had changed and had become prayer, composure in the disallowed sense of surrender, of a solemn protest. One could almost say that he had prayed in the same manner in which he wrote poetry, without a definite end or conclusion in mind. But rather writing was a process of conception in which even the most ordinary aspects of God were brought to expression. The rapturous excess that he had faulted himself for—the deliberate selection of that which had poetical effect in the "red violence" that some called life—completely vanished from these verses, and he turned decidedly toward the earthly as that which is near to God and which God manifests as his home. Here one is reminded of a tone that is sounded late in the *Elegies* in praise of the hereafter — the otherworldly angel estranged from the earth.

Earth, beloved, I will! Anonymous I affirm you!

Such was the contentment of the poet at home in Russia, as he described it four years later (Aug. 10, 1904, from Rome):

> That Russia is my home belongs to those grand and secret certainties from which I derive life....
>
> In Paris I did not come close to giving expression to Russia, and yet I think that somehow in Rome, in the face of antiquity, I am preparing for things Russian and later on, to return there.

In addition to Russian piety, a second aspect of Russia made a deep impression on Rilke because it clearly illustrated the hardship and labor that reminded him of his own personal experience. This is the course of Russian history, the peculiarity of a development between opposing forces — a growth that is stunted because of its (Russia's) geographical position between East and West, and, because it is burdened on both sides, it can only hope to create a synthesis within this paralysis. He did not tire of finding this in images, and one felt that he identified with such images. Indeed, action toward the outside would occur at the expense of the driving forces of his internal movement. This internal life demanded both patience and endurance in order to prepare him for the expression of his self in the future, an expression quite different from the power play of competition. He reflects on this in a letter from Oberneuland on Aug. 15, 1903:

> Perhaps the Russian is preordained to let history pass him by, so that later he will immerse himself in the harmony of things with his singing heart. He has only to endure, to hold out and, like the violinist who has not yet received his cue, to sit carefully holding the instrument in the orchestra, so that no ill befalls him… Filled more and more with greater internal affirmation I harbor an affection for this vast holy land within me.

The sentiment Rilke expressed here related to two things that no doubt characterized the Russian and his country. A mood surrounded him there for which the lust for power without question meant something quite different than for the Western European. Specifically, it was an affliction or an offensive temptation, a breach of that brotherhood that for the Russian embodies homeland and suspends him from needy isolation. What the Europeans regarded as a weak, sickly characteristic completely paralyzing the will to live is for this people a natural expression of certain strength, because they value the equality of people before God and not differences in the achievement of earthly goals. What is normally considered an extrinsic value is expressed here as something essential. The expanse of the Russian countryside into two parts of the world divests the notion of homeland from restrictive boundaries that presuppose the distances of one country from another. One would no sooner intentionally stray from the homeland than from the human community that ensures the union with one's kin. Between the White and the Black seas, from the shores of the Volga in the south to the birch forest in the north, Rilke encountered in some sense the same human being; and even the most common illiterate farmer had made the same pilgrimage through the grand expanse to visit a holy shrine or to locate displaced relatives scattered over all four corners of the earth. Two characteristic moments from that time remain clearly impressed in my memory. The first was the expression on Rilke's face in answer to a peasant girl's question: "How many times twenty-four hours is it from where you came from?" And the other was the expression on his glowing face after his first stay in one of the Volga villages, when a peasant woman bade him farewell and kissed him with the words: "You too are only one of the folk."

Even as an artist he was stimulated only by that which was truly human, in the same way that the great poets had impressed him as "Russian people." He was surrounded by a people who were artistically inclined in their fantasy and in their attitude toward life, and who had a primitive sense of the internal connection of poetry and life. Here artistic pursuits were not totally divorced from other human and more naive endeavors. Such were the impressions that rejuvenated him and made him more childlike. And, as such, they were the prelude to a confident beginning. Even when they led him now and then to overestimate particular Russian artists, they had the effect of impressing him with a sense of humanity that freed him to do his own work.

Everything that he undertook after his return from Russia was influenced by this. The fact that during the following year he established a house and family seemed to represent a secure, peaceful beginning that was reinforced by a community of artists and by the friendship of one man in particular, Heinrich Vogeler. Because Rilke met his wife, Clara Westhoff, one of Rodin's students, in Worpswede, he decided to settle down in nearby Westerwede.

But his work did not blossom there, and his anxiety returned. From Oberneuland-bei-Bremen where his daughter, Ruth, was raised by his in-laws, he complained (July 25, 1903):

> Lou, that pre-Wolfratshaus feeling, that you share,
> is still strong in me and I think I have not yet
> conquered it.

Meanwhile, his little Worpsweder book had appeared in 1902, but in retrospect he viewed even that with dissatisfaction:

> Even more than the Rodin book, it remained for me
> a mission of sorts, even as I wrote it. There were so
> many obstacles and limitations in the subject matter
> alone. The painters it depicted are only one-sided as
> artists and inclined toward things of marginal impor-
> tance. And since I tried to love them, they slipped
> through my hands; only the countryside remained.
> And so it helped that I was forced by the given pre-
> text to give voice to many things. And so much was
> written into those lines that had its origins in the days

of confusion and had been until then repressed into oblivion and formlessness.

His enjoyment of the artist colony soon withered. He lost his enthusiasm for the human community that he had depended on and that from his Russian experience had seemed an indispensable foundation for him:

> No art can come of this. And I am frightened to death of the superficial modesty of this life. — Kramskoi felt this way, as the children came and brought with them the present and concern for the immediate future instead of the most distant future. Here all substance is postponed. What is remote is no longer important, only yesterday; and tomorrow is more than eternity.

He was overwhelmed with the fear of being unable to begin:

> …where is the craft in my art, the deepest and most minute spot where I can begin to be proficient? I want to take every road back to the beginning. Everything that I have created will be nothing, smaller than the dusting on the threshold through which the next guest carries a trace of the road.

In this letter (Aug. 8, 1903, from Oberneuland) the desire for his actual calling tears free from everything else; it seeks its own expression:

> Isn't it true, Lou? It has to be so. We should be like a stream and not wander into canals and carry water

into the pastures? Isn't it true, we should hold our-selves firmly together and roar? Perhaps when we are old we will be permitted to spread ourselves out and empty into a delta ... dear Lou!

It troubled him deeply that he could not fulfill responsi-bilities that he had assumed and that he was a source of sup-port for no one:

> I used to think it would be better, if I would one day have a house, a wife and a child, things that were real and undeniable. I thought that I would become more visible, more palpable, more real. But, see, Wester-wede was real. I really did build my own house and everything that was in it. But it was an external reality and I did not live and expand within it. And now that I no longer have that little house and its lovely quiet rooms, I know that there is a person still there. And somewhere a child in whose life nothing is closer than he and I. This gives me a certain assurance and the ex-perience of many simple and deep things, but it does not give me the feeling of reality, that sense of equal worth, that I so sorely need: to be a real person among real things.

> 1904, from Rome

From the previous year came the self-recrimination:

> My house was nothing more than a strange woman for whom I was supposed to work and the people close to me are nothing more than visitors who do

not want to leave. Oh how I lose myself each time I want to be something for them. How I leave myself and can not come to them and I am on route between them and me. It's as if I were traveling to an unknown destination and I do not know where I am or how much of me is really there and within reach.

The same person who wrote those lines knew like no other man of the internal bonds that unite people. The same artistic disposition that inhibited his surrender to the group also heightened his awareness and made him more sensitive to the gentle claims and subtle needs of humanity. This painful contradiction was expressed in countless ways, and the urgency of this tension imbued his letters with an immediate presence that refused to succumb to resignation in the face of life. One such illustration of that refusal was the reunion of Rilke and his wife, Clara, with little Ruth at the home of his in-laws (recounted in a letter from Oberneuland, July 25, 1903):

> When we first arrived, we tried to be very still and pretended to be objects, and Ruth sat there and looked at us for a long time. Her serious dark eyes didn't stray from us and we waited for an hour without stirring, just as one waits for a bird to draw nearer, that the slightest movement would scare away. And finally she approached us and said a few words to see if we understood. And then when she came quite close she recognized her small brilliant reflection in our eyes and she cried out and smiled. That was her

first moment of intimacy.

And she patiently tolerated our shy attempts to be close to her and to share everything with her. And all at once it was natural to say "mother" and then, in recognition, she stretched out her arms and came toward us, as if toward love. And now she responds quite well to us. She calls me "man" and "good man" and is content that I am still there.

That painful contradiction that had separated Rilke in isolation from the community and that tore him to pieces in loneliness tormented him with the greatest anxiety during his first stay in Paris. If I do not fully quote from the descriptions of that time documented in the correspondence, it is because they have been very literally rendered in the Parisian diary of *Malte Laurids Brigge*. He introduces them with the words:

I want to tell you, Lou, that Paris was for me an experience similar to military school. Then I was gripped with fear, just as now I am terrified by what in unspeakable confusion is called life. Back then when I was a boy among boys, I was alone among them and oh, how alone I was among these people, how continually negated I felt by everything that I encountered. The coaches drove right through me. And people in a hurry made no detour around me. Full of hate, they ran over me, as if over a fault in the road in which old water has collected.

Worpswede, July 18, 1903

In those frightening and masterful portraits of the poorest of the poor, their illnesses, their fears, and their homelessness, it is as if the observer himself dissipates into the masses of people, becomes the ghost inhabiting their bodies and dies with them. Pity did not cry out from the enormity of those impressions; but, rather, Rilke, the observer, penetrated experience as in a rape that symbolically exposed his own despair: and in the midst of this horrible dying, the artist stood erect and "created"; he drew death into his symbolism. This transpired in direct opposition to the selfhood that had been allowed to emerge with the Russian people: in Russia something had led him to retreat into a forgotten trust of primal childhood, although the building was being erected without it already having been begun. Here one witnesses the development of the artist through the mounting human struggles and the impediments of the anguished soul: in this way the soul becomes creative. Rilke hardly wanted to acknowledge the identity, from which he heard his own fears cry out too loudly:

> Had I been able to create the fears that I experienced,
> I would have been able to make "things" out of them,
> real quiet things, that produce joy and freedom in
> their making and consolation in their existence, as if
> nothing had happened to me. But these fears that I
> suffered every day triggered hundreds of other fears,
> and they conspired against me and I could not tran-
> scend them. In struggling to give expression to them,
> I became creative. Instead of making them "objects"

of my will, I was only able to give them their own life that, in turn, tormented me and pursued me far into the night. If only my life had been better, quieter and friendlier; had my study protected me and had I remained healthy, perhaps I could have succeeded in objectifying my fear.

Once I was able to do this, if only for a short time, when I was in Viareggio. The anxieties returned in fuller force than before and overwhelmed me. But something happened. Prayers were conceived there, Lou, a book of prayers. I tell you, because my first prayers rest in your hands — prayers that I have thought of so often and that guarded me from the distance. Because they ring out so grandly and because they are at peace in your keep (and because no one besides you and me know of their existence), I could trust in them.

You see, I am only a stranger and a beggar. And I will pass away. But everything that could have been my home, had I been stronger, will rest in your hands.

During his first stay in Paris, he met Auguste Rodin through his wife, Clara. From the very first moment the impression was decisive for him. Rodin, after all, came to embody for Rilke the preeminence of the artist above all else. In retrospect, he describes those first impressions (1903):

When I first came to Rodin and breakfasted amongst strangers at his table in Meudon, I realized immediately that his house meant nothing to him, a small miserable necessity, perhaps a shelter from the rain, a roof overhead for periods of sleep; it concerned him not in the least and it placed no burden on his loneliness and composure. Deep inside himself he carried the darkness, refuge and peace of a house over which he himself became the sky and the surrounding forest, the vast expanses and the mighty stream that always overflowed.

He admitted with equal authority:

His daily life and the people who belonged to it, lay there like an empty bed through which he no longer flowed. But that in itself was not sad: for nearby one heard the great thunder and the powerful course of the stream that did not diverge into two arms.

And I think, Lou, this is how it must be; this is one life and that is another, and we are not made to have two lives.

Rilke and his wife finally left their home in Westerwede and settled in Paris to be with Rodin:

… for we wanted to learn how to work from him. We wanted only our work, and both of us wanted only to be at peace in our work and not be bothered by society.

And for the first time in years a light tone of heartfelt joy and surprise could be heard in Rilke's voice, as he told of how Rodin had taken him in and installed him as his secretary in a small house adjacent to the larger one in Meudon. While he handled the correspondence "in a French for which there must be a purgatory," he wished (in spite of his appointed duties) to emulate Rodin's primary commitment to his calling, echoed in the motto: "*Qu'il faut travailler, travailler toujours.*" ("It is necessary to work, to work always.")

The continuous process of the sculptor's craft enables him to work at any time without respect to the personal inclination to do so, because reality never totally vanishes in the material and is never solely dictated by a particular mood. Thus Rilke concluded that only through abandoning "sentiment" could he become fully engaged with the object —that only in such a way could he best serve the creative work that lay before him.

As early as 1903, after his short-lived friendship with Rodin, Rilke wrote from Oberneuland:

> For him what he sees and embraces with his eyes is always the sole thing, the world in which everything happens. If he forms a hand, it is there alone in space and it is nothing more than a hand. And God made only one hand in six days and poured water around it and arched a sky above it. When all was completed, he was at peace with it and it was a miracle and a hand.

The book about Rodin, together with the second one that emerged from Rilke's lectures on Rodin in Germany, depict so convincingly the originality of such a mode of work; here, instead of being pursued by inspiration, the objects present themselves to the tools so that further penetration becomes superfluous. What his letters contain on this subject was beautifully complemented in conversations we had. He expresses deep gratitude that the magnificent fruit of the New Poems could never have ripened without the support and protection of the giant tree of Rodin.

Even in 1911, after things had gone badly, he still recalls with fervor the blessed influence from that time (28 December, from Schloss Duino):

> I recall not with shame my best experiences in Paris, the time of the New Poems. I had expected nothing and nobody, and the whole world confronted me as a task to be performed and I answered confidently and clearly with pure achievement. How is it possible that now, when I am more educated in expression than ever, I remain lost, without a calling—superfluous?

Still though, the elusive quality of his achievements continued to trouble him. In 1904 from the Villa Strohl-Fern, he described the Roman spring:

> Now I observe everything so patiently and peacefully and I am able to learn. I feel that this is a form of progress and preparation; but you know, my gains are somehow like light convalescent steps forward, unusually weightless, unsteady and in need of constant support.

In fact he was in the process of becoming "educated in expression" and becoming a master of his own art. The early faint-hearted romanticism and the later confident stance toward reality now gave way to a complete surrender to an objectivity that found expression in reality and in its poetic refinement. But one condition actually did pose a threat to the necessary and important pursuit of his goal: the diametrical opposition of both artistic worlds that potentially led to great internal confusion. The palpable presence of the plastic material lends a constancy to the sculptor's mode of work, beyond the discontinuous inspiration, and the work acquires a tangible reality. For the poet, the equivalent is the *word* — possessing something of reality, capable of being apprehended by the senses, something broadly derived, a mere sign that serves practical and logical understanding. First, he must make it the material of poetry. The preparedness of the senses with which Rilke for weeks observed the panther in the Parisian *Tiergarten* or a plant in the Luxembourg Gardens was only the stage on which the new practical behavior unveiled itself. "Practical," in this sense, meant the penetration of what was emotionally colored to a depth of sympathetic understanding. This understanding suspended sentimental identification and allowed the work itself, the exterior sign, to speak for itself and become an oath, a creation. And years later Rilke was still trying to explain his failure and the severe repercussions that those days had wrought for him, in light of that distinction. He wrote in 1914:

> It occurs to me that the intellectual appropriation of the world that is primarily visual, as was the case with

me, is far less dangerous for the graphic artist, because it renders tangible results.

From the very beginning, in 1903, he was aware of the impediments to emulating Rodin successfully:

> I suffered from a superior example that could exercise no direct influence on my art. I actually experienced the physical pain of not being able to render a bodily form. That anxiety (its material content was the nearness of something too hard, too stone-like, too great) arose from the incompatibility of two artistic worlds.

Something other than just the incompatibility of two artistic worlds is called into question here. And Rilke alludes to that something peculiarly in his parenthetical remark: it was the opposition of character types. Rodin undoubtedly epitomized masculinity. Despite the power with which he surrendered himself to his art—and this is precisely what made him so significant for Rilke—he possessed his art and not vice versa. That is to say, that he was able to segment his being in such a way that he could relinquish almost everything to his art and yet could rejoice in what was left over, without requiring in all this a unifying focal point. And in the event that this process of creation shifted too far in either direction and became destructive and silencing, he could quite easily correct the situation by moving to the other side. To understand this, one had only to observe Rodin: the squat, stark naked, defier of the senses and the intellect. A peculiar brute force, empowered by an uninhibited spirit, emanated from him. Rilke had another kind of manliness that adhered to a totality and that manifested its creative power in the unity of both sexes; whatever was left over meant a rupture or loss of some kind, because the work always was more important for him than the man. Surely all creativity is only another name for the clash of a dual sexuality within us. But the gradations of sexuality are different and one can understand how the masculine moment in intellectual creativity is, by virtue of its freer structure, the more important and dominant one. It invests the external corporeal form with its power, whereas the female element can lead to a schism of the body and mind, as in an indescribable longing for pregnancy.

In any case, the deeper difference in their natures erupted and almost severed the wonderful bond between them. And, in the final analysis, Rilke may have lacked sufficient understanding of his great and different friend; he wanted Rodin to be as he in gratitude and admiration, and as he needed him for himself. There is no taking without its respective giving, if the gift is to be truly appreciated. Here, the youth had not given enough—the youth to whom Rodin had revealed the secrets of his age, his despair over the decline of sensual and artistic pleasure. There was something moving in the way that the old man, in Rilke's words, embodied the failings of age:

> One of the most important figures, a symbol far
> beyond his times, an uncommon example, a wonder

visible in the distance, and yet nothing more than an unspeakably lonely old man, alone in his great old age.

1903

In a letter already cited from 1911, one senses the absence of a final kindness for Rodin, as Rilke recalls with great compassion the injustices suffered by Rodin in his last years:

> I have gone through so much confusion, like the experience of seeing Rodin wronged in the seventieth year of his life, as if all his eternal work had not existed. And the same frivolous pettiness with which he brushed aside the greetings of passers-by still lurked in him and now playfully overwhelmed him and made his age grotesque and ridiculous. What do I do with these memories?

Following the first signs of a cooling in their relationship, Rilke at last began to do the right thing: he summoned his strength and applied the incredible training he had acquired to the work at hand. This resolve influenced the writing of his first prose work, *Malte Laurids Brigge*. From Rome (the Villa Strohl-Fern) on May 12, 1904, he reported:

> … My new book (its air-tight prose is an education for me and surely a step forward, that had to come, so that I could later write everything else — even the military novel)…

The military novel, the descriptions of his impressions at

St. Pölten, was his second priority. The first was his mastery of the most remote dark memories of childhood that he had always lacked the courage to exorcise. He called this "reliving his childhood" and to him this meant a descent into his true material that he had not yet confronted with his newly gained objectivity. And this impartial fearless objectivity that openly embraced the virgin ground of life itself necessitated a deeper tumult than mere "sentiment." He spoke of this to me. On one occasion in Paris we sat in his marvelous refectory at the Sacre Coeur, which had been furnished by Rodin, and which looked out onto a large terrace. The blossoming scent of early summer wafting in from the abandoned wild garden surrounded him as it had during those weeks of arduous work. He spoke of an enchantment with form that had almost led him to confuse life with the characters and episodes of his work. He also spoke of the persistent pressure that he felt because, in spite of it all, he had not recreated his childhood but rather he had eluded it and substituted a fiction in its place. I will never forget his eyes looking out into the summer as he intoned: "You see, it's like a fairy tale in which someone bewitched falls into a well at midnight. And for three whole days the hour of deliverance strikes. In vain. Where would courage come from?"

The struggle for this courage is the unspoken theme of the Malte book. The silence is broken in his questioning of the unrequited love of the God of *The Book of Hours*. That God holds man in a reassuring embrace. In contrast, the streets of Paris had seemed populated by fear, poverty, misery, corruption, and the God-forsaken. Now he summoned the strength to face that reality as well as the sinister spiritual effects of repressed memories. The complete love of God dispels not only fear but also that love that requires a response because the state of oneness denies any such opposition. And life is derived from this fact alone.

What Rilke had realized earlier in his attitude toward the material of his craft seeks here an internal confirmation, a deeper relation beyond the peripheral reward of sentiment. But in the attempt to achieve this final remove, the depth of his need does not come down to God. A consequence of this distance is that from now on that which is sacred seems removed from life and acquires a quiet otherworldliness — until the angels of the *Elegies* break through longing and despair and stand in God's place. They too do not return love, only differently: not out of oneness with the worshipper, but rather out of otherness. They do not share in the delight that they evoke. For this reason the *Elegies* are elegy; for this reason they commence with a cry of need: "Who, if I cried out, would hear me in the ranks of the angels?" But, at the same time, this is the joyful cry of the consummate artist. It is no longer a question of his existence, should need consume the one whom it clutches. Unity is achieved in the work itself; the angels are *created*.

Thus the Malte book appears to be illuminated with lightning flashes of hope and horror, pronouncements issued in a storm. The personal element still retraces its tracks into discovery. The impersonal character of its insights sheds light on the breadth of lived experiences of those real days. An indescribable clarity with which the poet is able to penetrate reality marks the changing psychic strata in which Rilke now lived. This was the twisting, rugged terrain on which he climbed and stumbled and picked himself up to pursue his path to God. A letter written much later (June 26, 1914, from Rue Campagne première, Paris) expresses it as follows:

> The more I examine it, it must be that I have one posture (the one to which I have educated myself in certain moments of work), and my soul has another, the next one, or the one next to that.
>
> And so I no longer serve it and nobody serves it. It is the bell-metal and God places it into the incandescence over and over again and prepares for the powerful hour of casting. But I am still the old form, the form of the previous bell, the obstinate form that has done exactly what it willed and does not want to be replaced — and so it remains uncast. How can I understand so much and still not be able to help myself?

Two years earlier (Schloss Duino, January 10, 1912) he remarked on how deeply troubled he was by this dilemma and how it prevented him from feeling whole:

> I am exhausted by this. I am like the cripple whose crutches wear through the coat's underarms. So too I fear that my worn-out one-sided nature will one day have holes and at the same time be new in other places.

When at the end of the book, the prodigal son returns home and realizes that he has not really returned home, that he is not at all the person that others perceive him to be, when joyful forgiveness presents no smaller misunderstanding than love that is reproving and angry, Rilke resurrects the self-image that he formulated in his letter. We see this in his coat that is "like new" and we don't know that indeed it was crutches that supported his weary body in the meantime. There is nothing left for him to do but to act as if he were not misunderstood, that is, to proceed as if in borrowed or illusory clothing. This at least protects his solitude and he is not driven to behave in a manner alien to himself. As the years passed, this became more and more characteristic of his experience. He allowed misunderstandings to go uncorrected in order to remain unrecognizable behind them. He was aware of this very early. In 1905, on the Feast of the Epiphany, he wrote from Oberneuland:

> When others feel themselves understood and totally accepted, I feel prematurely torn from some sort of hiding place.

He regarded what we call "fame" in a like manner. Nobody ever reacted to fame with more awareness and less vanity. But, on the other hand, fame, that broad rumor of familiarity, had also its more felicitous side effects, similar to the misunderstandings mentioned above. Fame was a convenient, comfortable form, a mere garment to be slipped on. He often spoke of how difficult and draining it had initially been for him to give of himself and to express himself without artifice and failure. For he felt the constraints of the given moment too strongly to accomplish that in a naive and unintentional manner. And so he withdrew as if from the stare of alien eyes, just as he hesitated to tell a story, to make an observation or offer a remark in an all-too-casual and offhand manner. This was the inborn artistry in him, that creative restlessness that permeated every pore of his being. It was also this that made him a first-rate storyteller and that made him able to transform even the most simple impressions and experiences into a unique and unforgettable event.

Meanwhile, the normal everyday routines in which Rilke was known to seek refuge did not simply offer comfort and relief, but rather a form of imprisonment, of seclusion. He recalled an early childhood experience in which the fright that accompanied this solitude was exquisitely manifest in the extreme. Dressed in a costume of his choosing, he sees his reflection in a full-length mirror. (There is a lingering concern that little Renee might come to life.) At first he is amused. Then he makes a face and his curiosity is piqued to know if he is still capable of recognizing himself through the disguise. Gradually, he is overcome by anxiety over the strangeness of this odd image. Finally, he is seized with such anger that, arms flailing, he vainly struggles to tear himself out of the disguise. Covered with sweat and choked with fear, he hurls himself to the ground and is prepared to die. This memory embraces the full ambiguity of the self's essence and its appearance, the duplicity of the outer shell that protects life and to which he ultimately must succumb in death.

But he was most profoundly aware of this danger when he recognized it in the midst of his creativity, when he stumbled upon it as if upon a tragic event that could not be rooted out of his consciousness and that as such had become part of the creative process. Reflecting on the Malte book (Dec. 28, 1911, from Schloss Duino) he made the following remarks:

Good Ellen Key[3] has naturally confused me with Malte and she has given up. But no one except you, my dear Lou, can determine if and to what extent he is like me. If he — in part the product of my fears — perishes simply to spare me from my own destruction, or if, through this portrait, I have fallen into a stream that snatches me away and consumes me. Can you understand that I have retreated behind this book and I am left behind like a survivor without resources, helpless to the core, and with nothing more to do? The closer I came to the end, the more strongly I felt that it would be an indescribable piece. I always believed that it would be a high watermark. But now it so happens that all the water has run off toward the old side and I sink in a drought that does not change. And were it only that: but the other one, nothing that was not in his hands and in his heart. He appropriated everything to the urgency of his despair. Nothing is new to me that I don't instantly discover the crack, the spot where it had been torn. Perhaps this book had to be written the way one ignites a mine. Perhaps I should have jumped back from it precisely at the moment of its completion. But I rely too heavily on property and I can not endure limitless poverty, as much as it may be my mission to do so. I have had enough ambition to invest my entire capital in a lost cause. On the other hand, its value first became evident in loss and consequently, the greater duration of Malte seemed to be not so much a period of decline but rather a peculiarly dark ascension into a neglected and remote part of the sky.

This heavenly region was so dark and remote because he had saved himself. He had not committed himself fully to that total impoverishment that might have redeemed him in its divine splendor instead of leaving him suspended in a state of tenuous reliance on it. So too he conceived his work as a form of externalization. What he exposed of his internal life was like a change of clothing that did not transform him but rather left him behind, feeling robbed and cold. There is also a hybrid aspect to the work itself that vacillates between appearance and being, freedom and oppression, death and life: and it is the final, most powerful expression of this duality. This can not be distinguished strongly enough from the character-schism and guilt that accompanies such development in other personalities—from that critical tension that completely polarizes its victims and renders the guilty repentant. In contrast, we are not concerned here with "good" and "bad" or that which is "sinful" or "ideal" (to use the popular terms) but rather with equal power against power, both possessing the same potential fate. A person does not succumb to this fate but exists in it, and so, in grousing about his own fate, he is. He suffers greatly. It's as if he were a snail that carries its house like a handicap and its loss in death could hardly be considered too dear a price to pay. But it would be equally good if the shell arched over him more splendidly than it ever could be itself. And the snail would be justified in giving its entire life's work to that secure union and its ornate roundness.

Rilke perceived his corporeality as just such an awkward abode; it was that aspect of the self that could not be subsumed in the creative process. As such it represented, in no ascetic or moral sense, an opposing force, a threat. It embraces the same creative principle, even if it is not interchangeable with the other. It still involves the same mirror image that casts a derisive reflection. Thus his corporeality becomes a kind of mimicry that temptingly misleads him. His complaints about physical problems that he reported so often and with such urgency in all his letters must be read as if he wrote about a much larger issue—the corporeal being that embodied for him his creative vision. He calls down each of his words from the cross on which he was violently nailed upright, until he has spoken all seven words (behind all seven words stands the single tortured utterance: "I thirst").

Entries in earlier and later letters attest to this concern:

> I agonize like a dog that limps with a thorn in its foot, and everywhere he goes he is no longer a dog but rather a thorn, something that he does not understand and that can not be understood....
>
> See, only three days of relative "well-being," i.e. my body's neutrality, and an inner power took hold and prevailed, instead of me being the one to drag around this power like a sick bird pulling the weight of his wings.

And from the first part of the same letter:

> In my condition which depended upon keeping the intellect in perilous abeyance and exposing it scrupulously to both heaven and earth, it (the intellect) lay so close to both, that the body in its hollow stupor drew from this attitude the worst possible example and made itself a monkey of the intellect, and in its own way, at the least prompting, it too became productive.
>
> July 4, 1914, Paris

> — A soul that is inclined to harmonize with the immense exaggerations of art must be able to rely on a body that does not mimic it, that is precise and never exaggerates. My body runs the risk of becoming the caricature of my intellect.
>
> January 20, 1912, Schloss Duino

And from March 16, 1912:

> Sometimes I feel as if I were approaching happiness
> and I stand before a flower that blossoms through an
> old stone wall and I am unable to draw nearer. I am
> left with the feeling of always waiting for happiness,
> and everything is suddenly diminished by the melan-
> choly of having once been able to achieve that joy. It
> is strange, Lou. On the contrary, I progress toward my
> own ruination that manifests itself with such vehement
> and relentless clarity. There is no end to it. By chance
> one evening not too long ago, I read the letter in
> which Montaigne reports the death of his friend de la
> Boetie. Afterwards, I cried so much, I could not sleep.

And on a page before that:

> My nature desires so strongly but I don't encourage
> it. There's something perverse in that. I am actually in
> collusion with the temptor and he employs me in his
> service to do the most vile things for which he can
> find no other.

From a letter already quoted:

> Routine, ordinary things, through which I used to
> find my way as if through a haze of bad air, become
> thicker and thicker. And I can imagine that one day
> they might close in on me like walls.

But the "walls" that surrounded him were his body: that

prison, which exposed and mocked him, created a boundary from that which was alien. At the same time this boundary kept him locked out, at bay, and raped him. In this state, he lay as if buried and rendered totally impotent. Only seldom does it seem to him:

> — I become real, I am. I take up space like an object. I weigh heavily and fall, and a hand comes and lifts me up. As part of the building of a larger reality, I feel myself supporting a deep foundation and I can feel the weight of what I carry on either side of me. But again and again after long hours of immersion, I am the stone that is tossed aside and is so weary that the grass of idleness has plenty of time to grow long on it.

> The hours of abandonment do not diminish but rather they lengthen and multiply. It terrifies me. If I lie there, who would find me under all that growth? And am I not already ground into dust and indistinguishable from the rest of the earth so that any one of the sad paths leading in all directions goes over me?

> 1903, Via del Campidoglio, Rome

The imagination of the prisoner attempts in vain to overcome death through a universal life wish, through which the walls are allowed to expand to desired fullness; what remains is the state of being inconsolable, explosively depicted in an excerpt from one of his notebooks that he once sent to me from Spain (Ronda, Feast of the Epiphany, 1913):

"Actually he was at last free and if something had prevented his death, it was surely only oversight. Hence, he, unlike the others, did not forge on (toward death) but could retreat. His experience was external to him; it lay in the concrete things with which children play and it died in those things. Or it was saved in the chance look of a stranger who passed by. At least then he would give himself over to fear. But the dogs also ran away with it, agitated and fearful that he would take it away from them. But when he walked before the almond tree that was in full bloom, he was terrified to find it so ripe, so overgrown and so entirely separate from him. Unable to position himself exactly opposite the tree, he despaired to find that it did not mirror his being. Had he become a saint, he would have found freedom from this condition, the external, undeniable joy of poverty; for perhaps Saint Francis lay there torn apart in the same way and then he was eaten and the whole world became the flavor of his being. But he had not peeled himself clean. He had not torn himself free and given away the pieces of his shell. He held them before an imaginary mouth (the way children do with puppets) and he smacked his lips without ever biting. He was like the peel, the residue that was left behind, however much he might have desired to be the sweetness of the fruit."

I wrote this early today in my notebook. You realize whom it concerns. Your letter arrived yesterday. Yes, the two elegies are there. But I can tell you that they are such a small and fragmented part of what was then in my power. Circumstances and forces like the onset of The Book of Hours — if only everything were not suspended?[4]

At the time of its conception *The Book of Hours* was not intended for publication, and it cost its author great labor before he decided to publish it five years later (1905). He had not looked at it for a couple of years, and after I sent it to him, he wrote from Worpswede:

It was a reunion to have the old black book in my hands. It is so interwoven with happiness, recognition, longing and gratitude, destruction and creation that it recreated the pregnant intensity of that other meeting that I recall.

The old prayers resounded again here in this gray cell. They sounded so unchanged. Once again I was the tower whose huge bells begin to toll, vibrating in the interior and trembling down to the foundation, reaching out beyond myself. Reaching to you. It was all so close to me, as if we stood face to face ... Oh how I long just once to feel the hand within me that throws the larks so high into the sky.

What came as complete surprise was that after the publication of *The Book of Hours* he thought that *Malte Laurids*

Brigge would be his last book. Sometimes he played with the idea and lived within it. The thought of being freed from the pressures of the creative process actually invigorated him. It meant freedom from the opposition of the mind-body struggle that thwarted his most natural instincts toward well-being.

> … if the thought not to write that so often dangled before his nose like a peculiar kind of relief had really been serious. You mustn't laugh, but for weeks toward the completion of *Brigge* I had the feeling I would later study and become a doctor somewhere in the country.

He wrote this toward the end of January in 1912 from Duino. During his youth he wanted to be a country doctor. "Country" represented harmony with nature, while "doctor" stood for unity with the townsfolk. Hence health and renewal become a real possibility.

But the first two elegies that he mentioned in the previous letter were also delivered into existence in 1912. And, hence, the poet's calling was saved as well. If one considers the length of time — almost two decades — that separated him from the completion of the elegies, one senses the deep toll that rang out against his chosen vocation; one senses the private meaning of "no longer wanting to write." In fact, the Malte book was a "high watermark." It embraced the decision to achieve the possibility of that immeasurable poverty, to deny his own harmony with nature and to sacrifice himself for the effect of his work on others.

One of Rilke's poems from the previous years was occasioned by a similar conflict between art and life: that is his "Requiem" to Paula Modersohn-Becker.[5] The fact that she was torn from her creativity into death, following the birth of a much wanted child, gave rise to Rilke's most profound questioning of life. Motherhood realized the creative unity of body and spirit but tore the woman from her creation, in the same way that, conversely, the sterile opposition of the body against ultimate spiritual consummation had almost forced Rilke to renounce his creativity. It was that mystery surrounding the female's fate that made all young girls his sisters: it was this and not, as was the popular facile interpretation, the girlish timidity of a young man, that made so many of his early songs to young girls resonate with such sweetness and deep melancholy. In the female's potential to procreate, to nurture, to protect, and to educate there lies a male drive that declares the hidden similarity of the sexes: both long for the act of birth, to express their most essential being in the life beyond the self.

The years following the Malte book are distinguished by Rilke's translations[6] that are concerned with the exaltation of women: *The Twenty-Four Sonnets of Louise Labe, The Portuguese Letters of Marianna Alcoforado*, and *The Love of Magdalen.* In those works he was drawn to that other female characteristic that he wished so strongly to claim as his own: namely, the ability to be thoroughly transported without consideration for oneself, as in the case of motherhood. The ability to be transported and to allow oneself to be consumed in love, to experience love as a monumental achievement that discloses its own wealth and against which the good fortune of being loved in return becomes almost petty. The fact of love itself without regard for its reward, requited love: this alone would rid creativity of its self-destructive element. This was pure creativity. For a long time he labored under Malte's conception of an "unloving God." Years later he wrote:

> You know of my planned discourse on God's mutual love.
> A note that I read somewhere brought to mind the wonderful connection that Spinoza must have posited through his insight into the separateness of those who love God from any notion of reciprocity on God's part. I didn't have to think any further than what lay there before me. What of Spinoza did I have to read in order to educate myself? If only you had the relevant volumes?

And so he was relieved of finding any more meaningful truth to this problem than that of Spinoza's philosophical stance or the eroticism of great lovers who succumbed totally to the object, without regard for a response. What impressed him so deeply was basically almost the opposite: love's violence not only destroyed mutual love but, one might say, it also negated the object itself. What is so vulgarly expressed in the misused philistine saying, "So what if I love you, what does it have to do with you?" can mean in its least selfless and least loving extreme, "Don't bother me with this." That is to say, it is similar to an object-free immersion in a self-referential play of fantasy. For the poet, this immersion represented the point of departure for his eroticism in art and a creativity that did not require a specific object but the entire cosmos to command his interest. As such, through a self-deceptive confusion, creativity acquires the meaning of a personal and human love of an object, and hence it seeks a response.

Often enough he acknowledged something unreal about his contacts with other people, especially the inclination to disclose too much of himself to others. In August of 1905 he wrote from Oberneuland:

> I have only one inner identity and I must either
> remain locked up (i.e. silent or rambling foolishly)
> or open myself up in such a way that this single
> inhabitant becomes visible. The flawed character of
> my inner self inhibits all intercourse, because in this
> form it can only lead to misunderstandings that force
> me into undesired relationships, from which I only
> suffer and experience dangerous setbacks. It is signifi-
> cant that I have won all my "friends" in this dishonest
> way, and consequently I possess them badly and with
> a bad conscience. For this was the only way that I
> could acquire a horde of friends who could give me
> nothing in return for my persistent efforts. No one
> can reciprocate, because I give recklessly and brutally
> without regard for the other. I unburden myself—

And in exactly the same tone, Dec. 28, 1911, from Duino:

> Dear Lou, it always goes badly when I wait for people,
> need them and seek out their company: it only fills
> me with gloom and guilt. You can not know how
> little effort I give to being with them....

He thereby underestimated what good came to him
through his social contacts. Even if they were only diver-
sions, they served the important function of directing his energies outward, instead of damming them up within himself.
A major part of his increasing hypochondria and his hyper-
sensitivity resulted from a feeling of abandonment in his
own body. He used the same expressions to describe the
feeling—the sensation of "being swollen," of the "easing of
tension," the "high swelling that contracted under a drop
of acid"; the sensitivity of the face (throat, forehead, eyes,
and neck) to this sensation. But each time a relationship tem-
porarily freed him from a physical and emotional immersion
in himself, it always came to the same end:

> Once again, after a long difficult period, I found my-
> self not replenished with strength and courage, but
> rather plagued to an extreme until it subsided and was
> purged (one can not easily emulate me)—

And again in 1915, he remarked:

> ... The painful certainty that every encounter will do
> violence to me, instills terror in me, induces me to flee
> and ends in a relapse into ruin and solitude.

Rainer Maria Rilke as a young poet, 1900

Rilke on the balcony of his Swiss retreat, Château de Muzot, in 1923, a year after he completed the *Duino Elegies*.

Lou Andreas-Salomé at the Congress of Psychoanalysis in Weimar, September, 1911, one of the early meetings of the founders of psychoanalysis. In the front row, from left: Mira Ginsburg, Lou Andreas-Salomé, Beatrice M. Hinkle and Emma Jung. Behind them, Hungarian analyst Sandor Ferenczi is directly behind Lou, Sigmund Freud stands in the center; Carl Jung is behind Emma Jung; Karl Abraham is on the far right.

Lou Andreas Salomé at age 73, just three years before her death
in February, 1937.

Yet as a sign of health there remains the irrepressible longing for human redemption and relief:

> … not to totally rid myself of its presence, but if only this loneliness were less oppressive, if it came into good hands, it might lose that air of malaise and I could experience it as something continuous instead of dragging it in the midst of the confusion like a bone from bush to bush.

But the possibility of changing his state depended upon a basic condition that could not be fulfilled. He realized very early that his poor choices and failures in judgment were not to be equated with a mere "weakness of the psychic sphincter muscle." Productive hours depended not only on undisturbed immersion in thought but rather on nothing less than the correct impressions that afforded the opportunity for such immersion. One could say (and this is all too often overlooked) that the creator finally encounters only that which his hours are inclined to conjure up and thereby places himself in an incomprehensible rapport with the most repressed and primal part of himself. This secret dependency disturbed Rilke, because he felt the constraints of this dependency and he dared not touch it with the oldest and most hidden possibilities of memory. *Les impressions, au lieu de me pénétrer, me percent* ("impressions, instead of penetrating me, pierce me"), he wrote, seized by this fear many years later. Earlier (July 25, 1903) he had described how external sensations were lost in him forever:

It falls, falls for years and finally I lack the strength to dredge it up from within. And I go around fearfully with it and never plumb my burdensome depths. — I … let my own harvest grow old and outlast itself.

Hence, his suspicion that in relationships he only sought to escape himself. And thus, the self-recrimination that they led him to deception and betrayal.

On the other hand, there loomed the constant danger that the impulse toward that arrested state of internal relief, toward the final harvest, would become its opposite and be transformed into chaos, the experience of immeasurable and incessant loss. He once poignantly depicted this state with the plaintive words (Paris, June 26, 1914):

I am like a little anemone that I once saw in my garden in Rome. It had opened up so wide during the day that it could not close during the night! It was terrible to see it in the dark meadow, wide open, still inhaling everything through its wide-open throat — with the much too imposing night above that would not be consumed. And nearby, the clever sisters, each closed up around its small body. I too am incurably exposed and vulnerable. For this reason I am totally distractible; I decline nothing. My senses respond to the least disturbance without asking my permission. If there is a noise, I give myself over to it and become that noise. And since everything responds to stimuli and wants to be stimulated, so I too want to be unsettled, and I am endlessly restless. Despite this public exposure some life has actually been preserved in me. It has retreated to an internal spot and resides there, the same way people live during a kind of occupation, in deprivation and worry. Should it make itself known, then it thinks better times have come, through fragments of the *Elegies* or a first line here or there, it always has to retreat, because there looms the constant threat of compromise and surrender. And between the uninterrupted strivings and struggles to achieve an unattainable internal existence, there lie rooms of healthy feeling, an empty wasteland, abandoned, cleaned out, an uninhabitable no man's land, the neutrality of which reveals why all pleasure from men and nature is squandered on me.

In January of 1912, he had already written from Schloss Duino:

How often it happens that I emerge like chaos from my room and I am seized by the presence of an outsider. I discover a style that actually belongs to that other. And in the next moment, to my astonishment, I articulate things so beautifully, while everything in my consciousness was completely amorphous.

Over the years the numerous and lengthy journeys represent the will to penetrate external impressions: Scandinavia, Italy, France, Spain, and Egypt. The Egyptian trip left a lasting impression, for he subjected himself to impossible inhuman conditions:

> … I've lost my home and support and I have ended up like one thrown by a runaway horse, left dragging in the stirrups.

In retrospect, he didn't see the humor in this and wrote a year later (Schloss Duino, March, 1911):

> … the trial through which I suffered this past year and which I imagine has caused my soul much damage, not because it was difficult but because it was false, not because it sapped my strength but because it distorted perspective …

He found it infinitely significant that nature reproached him through its own creations:

> When a yellow Kabyle dog attacked me in Cairo, south of Tunis, and bit me (it was the first time ever in my life that a dog had reacted this way for no reason), I had to admit that he only expressed in his own way that I was completely in the wrong with everything and everyone around me.

For longer stays Rilke often lived in castles, fortresses, and towers: this occurred partly by accident, due to friendships that afforded him this form of refuge, but he was also inclined to take up residence in such places. This has been all too often misconstrued to mean that Rilke welcomed contact with old lines of nobility. In fact, it had to do with other needs, such as the need for a safe enclosure, to an extent, a kind of trap, in which one is instantly suspended without having to create a covering. Symbolism played a role here too: what had endured for so long and possessed its own unforgettable meaning gave him a certain peace and suspended his sense of abandonment, in the same way that the history of known family lines in certain individuals seemed more readily available to him and hence it seemed easier to replicate. But this too shared the dual character of the "trap"—that everything that was secure was also imprisoned—and set constraints on him. Even from Duino, the beloved birthplace of the first *Elegies*, he writes that he is held like a prisoner within its immense walls (1911). He was also constantly driven to flee and plagued with increasing anxiety that what had initially announced itself at Duino would never achieve a breakthrough. A decade would pass before that happened. In 1911 he wrote from Duino:

> The frightening thing about art is that the further one comes in art, the more one is committed to extremes, to what is almost impossible.

While he was in Göttingen, he entered the following words into my diary:

> —let it be necessary to experience that greatness is not overexertion, but rather nature.

And on another day he wrote the verse:

> Will there be no next time for me? Should I
>   simply tarry?
> (So often my cry destroys and my laughter distorts);
> but sometimes in the glow of the light flame
> I recognize my interior heart.
> That which achieved such internal spring,
> even as it passed through the cellars of life.
> Oh how it braved the greatest pathways,
> climbed and like a star understood what had
>   become night.

In the fall of 1913, during our stay in the Riesengebirge (where we had traveled from Munich via Hellerau), I discovered that he had entered into my diary an observation from Goethe's *Italian Journey*:

> For we sense the frightful conditions under which only the true naturals can realize the ultimate possibility of achievement.

More hopeful letters came from time to time. Or if they did confess gloomier thoughts, they always closed with a word that betrayed a self-contented smile:

> So now your old mole has once again burrowed a trench for you and cast dark soil right across a perfectly good road. I say such intimate things to you, like the people in the Old Testament, an entire volume of sayings: for that which stands in the burning

briar of your life—that is exactly what must command me as well.

In July, 1914, Rilke stayed for a time in Göttingen, and I can still remember the hours we enjoyed together. His big eyes would narrow and a genuine humor would surface, full of childlike charm that delighted the heart. We awoke at an ungodly early hour, wandered barefoot through the dewy meadows, just as we had done in the days of Wolfratshausen. That July was clear and hot, rich in berries and roses, and bathed in sunlight.

The fact that Rilke had come over from Paris perhaps saved him from the danger of internment. (His personal effects were seized in Paris. They were partially returned to him ten years later.)[7]

War broke out.

Rilke had gone to visit his publisher in Leipzig, and I had gone to Munich where we were to meet again. At the outbreak of the war, I assumed that he would not be able to leave and so I took the last train home. He assumed the same of me and rushed forth. And so we passed each other (in transit) going in opposite directions.

In his youth Rilke had been classified as "unfit for military service."[8] After the second or third time he had reported for duty, a telegram came to Wolfratshausen with the message, "Free and once again happy." But in the course of the war, he enlisted, although he never saw active duty because he collapsed during drills and was subsequently assigned to work in the press office in Vienna.

The war made an impression that never left him. When he longed to reconstruct the past and thereby master it for a new future, he was confronted with an equally strong feeling that it must be forgotten, if reality were not to assume a ghostly aura. Hence, Rilke depicts the impressions evoked by his return to Venice where he had stayed with the Prince and Princess von Thurn-und-Taxis and then with [Eleanora] Duse before the war:

> My wish to find everything unchanged, was so liter-
> ally fulfilled, that it seemed as if I stood on the edge,
> over the unspeakable years, as if it were in this pecu-
> liar way possible to experience once again the mere
> repetition of what had been: but the heart, suspended
> during the war years, suffered the guilt that its life
> and its exterior had remained unchanged and it expe-
> rienced all that was old in the same unchanged fash-
> ion. Endless repetition set in and nearly filled me with
> anger when I saw it from a distance. When I then, by
> chance, discovered that Duse had arrived ill and
> sought refuge in Venice, it seemed that even this
> would repeat itself from one day to the next; I left
> and returned to Switzerland.

Nothing horrified him more than the fact that he succumbed to overwhelming impressions through a "suspension of the heart" that left him incapable of feeling. He complains about this still in 1919 (January 13, from Munich):

Dear, dear Lou, I am so out of sorts. My inner self has retreated and protects itself and reveals nothing. My resistance to stimuli from the outer world is so great that not only the war but even nature's innocence and purity have no effect on me. Never before have I been so immune to the wind, to trees, to the night's stars. Since I have had to witness this in the evil guise of an infantry uniform, I have experienced a peculiar sense of estrangement — that unrelatedness that I found necessary to describe back then in order to spare myself destruction.

Here a personal quality supervenes in Rilke's capacity for human suffering. The infantry uniform belongs not only to the war years but to the period he spent in military school. This was a time that he had never recalled, and the secret influence of those dark memories was something that he vehemently denied. The "return to sameness" in Venice derived its paralyzing and frightful effect from the notion that something inaccessible and past could reveal itself as present, as if that unfulfilled abyss — life itself — did not lay between then and now. And at the same time the quaking uncertainty persists — the tremulous longing to unite that which is conjured up with actual life, as if this alone might release life from damnation and life might be redeemed in the courage of creativity.

He struggled with this problem even after he had settled in Switzerland and it disrupted his work. He complained of this from the Château de Muzot in 1921: "An incredible inability to concentrate has resulted from the interruption of the war years."

The war must have precipitated an unprecedented flood of past experiences, for he had more and more magnanimously forgotten how to do one thing: namely, to identify the external world as the guilty party. This was most painful for him. At that time we experienced so fully the real surrender to the outside world and the violence that peoples inflicted upon each other. During the war's third winter and spring that we spent together in Munich, the intensity with which this fate afflicted him became with each day more and more clear to me. And even so, I think that he was a bit further along than we were and I at least observed this in one principal area. What he had suffered through in years of agony, he had somehow appropriated from the deepest suffering of the times. For—beyond all the differences of opinion and nationality—was it not just such a shattering internalization that made us human? Was it not something totally singular and personal, internalized in everyone, in all peoples? Was it not the extent to which any individual (in his thought and his action) acknowledged what was happening and yet at the same time wished to feel himself blameless in the face of those deeds? The insight that we are humans capable of doing this to each other [making war] casts both the victims and the perpetrators of the crime together. It summons forth each man and forces without distinction everyone to shoulder responsibility under the heavy weight of conscience; it humbles and clarifies our naive self-satisfaction and reduces the joy in ourselves to an indispensable minimum that almost touches our core. Now after such a long time, there he stood ready—he, whose efforts to creatively embody his fictional faces had given rise to the dark knowledge of what it was to be human, and it hurled him into greater depths than one ordinarily plumbs. He struggled on the boundaries of what was humanly possible and with greater determination pressed toward its chasms. His silence was perhaps the most eloquent expression of this experience.

At this juncture I come to that which explains the nature and scope of Rilke's influence on others. Why he, so often plaintive and directionless himself, could seem a source of advice and assistance to others, a leader, without whom an entire community would have considered itself deprived and orphaned. The reason for this was that still out of the holes and scraps of his own raggedness an internal grandiosity was exposed that was especially appealing, in that it inspired one with courage. Nothing would be more counterfeit and inaccurate than to reconstruct an image of Rilke primarily from his lamentations and from his self-loathing. One must constantly bear in mind that it was his extraordinary artistic sense that threatened his stability and well-being. But also his human side, apart from the purely poetic, was sketched in broad strokes. His humanity was "full of spirit" and so permeated with intellect and wit that it frequently carried Rilke to completely remote areas of meaning. This was expressed most convincingly in the early years just beyond boyhood when his poetic ability exploded now and then in a superabundance of feeling. Whoever spoke to him then at greater length surely must have come away with that impression. He himself experienced this as a dissatisfaction with himself, as a hunger for understanding and knowledge of the first order. And this manifested itself both in his exact mastery of chosen fields of study as well as in a more Faustian motivation. (Already in the early letters he listed those areas requiring his immediate attention: "history, physiology, biology, experimental psychology, anatomy, not to forget Grimm's dictionary." On another occasion: mathematics, the study of Arabic, old languages in general, and, more specifically, the study of antiquity from an art-historical perspective, as well as the works of the medieval mystics.) If it pained him bitterly not to become especially proficient in those subjects, it was because he did not want to approach his studies as an avocation but as a singular goal. From the beginning he believed that there was nothing that did not serve creativity, just as the craftsmanship in sculpture was secured for the first time in the work itself.

> Does craftsmanship lie in language itself, in a better understanding of its inner life and will, its development and past history? —
>
> Does it lie in any particular study, in the more exact knowledge of something? — Or does it lie in a certain, well-established and inherited culture? ...
> But—I must be wary of all that is inherited, and my achievements are so small.

1903, from Oberneuland

With obvious discomfort he senses how creativity and learning both need and yet oppose each other, and that this realization was often an impediment to learning. When he was plagued with doubts and did not advance, he believed himself to be awkward and bungling:

> As if I had to return through some unborn knowledge on a weary path of twists and turns.
>
> Oh, if only I had workdays, Lou, if only my most secret heart chamber were a workplace, a cell, and refuge for me; if only this monkishness in me were the foundation of a cloister around my work and worthy of devotion. If only I could lose nothing more and erect everything around me according to kinship and importance.
>
> If only I were redeemed, Lou! For I am fragmented and disintegrating like a dead man in an old grave. —
>
> Then I would have so much to do that one work-day would resemble the next, and I would have work that was always successful, because it would begin with that which is attainable and small and yet grand in its conception.

His creative drive and his knowing spirit, always standing in the way, are united in him as one longing humanity that wants to merge and wants nothing more than to confirm this alliance in every moment:

> I know that I can not extricate my life from the fates

with which it has been intimately bound up; but I
must find the strength to lift it entirely as it is with
everything into a peace, into a solitude, into the quiet
of deep days of work. Only there will I find all that
you have promised me....

Oberneuland, Aug. 11, 1903

From this irrepressible desire for homogeneity, which
also embraced his artistry, there arose an incredible con-
scientiousness. He, who felt too presciently to be torn by
conscience, by its punishing weight or its liberating relief,
devoted himself to a kind of preparedness. He focused on
the hour of productivity that is impossible to command but
necessary to obey. His ethos—to interject a misused word—
embraced this readiness as a conception that could occur
to him anywhere and at any time, provided that nothing
strange or hostile preoccupied him or posed a hindrance and
distraction.

From Sweden (Furuborg, Jonsered, on Oct. 19, 1904) he
had written:

If my life is to become better, I must concentrate on
two things: power and conscience—I must learn to
work. I told myself this for years and continue to
dabble. Hence, my suspect conscience; so much more
suspect when others trust me.

This sensitivity increased with his inability to still his
conscience, like an actor who achieves his desired goal in

action. If he had been able to pray, as a child prays to an earthly father who gives him a favorable hearing, he would have prayed for nothing more than to be present and always recognized in "his father's house." For him there was only this or homelessness. For Rilke there was no hierarchy of values, nor were there special values suited for the artist; the value of values had to apply to the artist as well. What set him apart from others was his steadfast pursuit of a singular and ultimate goal: the realization of the artist within himself. And this pursuit posed in all seriousness the extreme question, when would he gain access to that artist? What distinguished him, beyond all artistic recognition, what still beamed from his forehead as he lay on the ground was this: there was never anyone who had more spiritual concerns than he.

And with the years his impatience increased:

> To begin again. Certainly, in school it helped to be able to turn over a new leaf in my notebook. This one now is so full of the most shameful mistakes, and in moments of abandon or reflection, there at last stood the right answer on a totally erased spot, on the little skin of a hole.
>
> Paris, rue Campagne premiére, Oct. 21 1913

Finally, there was no misery, even the most gruesome kind, that he did not take upon himself in order to succeed; for a long time he had ceased to fear that misery. A year and a half earlier (from Duino, March, 1912) he had noted:

I used to marvel at the saints who purposefully subjected themselves to bodily abuses. Now I understand that this passion for pain, even in the torture of martyrdom, represents the haste and impatience to no longer be interrupted and disturbed by the evil that can come from this side (meaning this life).

The same letter reads:

Many a day I view creation with the worry that at any moment pain can erupt and cause it to cry out, so great is my fear of the body's abuse of the soul that achieves peace in the animals and safety in the angels.

It is the body that does not allow itself to be part of the desired unity, resists it and is hedged between the animal and the angel (Paris, June 26, 1914):

My body has become like a trap, a surface of traps in which tortured impressions perish, a rigid intractable region; and far far away, as in the middle of a cold star, that wonderful fire can volcanically erupt, here and there, under appearances that, like devastation, are confusing and dangerous to the indifferent surfaces.

The invincible and enduring nature of that part of the self that remains external and foreign in relation to inner experience summoned forth a melancholy in Rilke that escalated into a complete renunciation of the physical. This is the point where the angel of his poetry appeared. It grew out of the craving for that which partook of the "peace in the animals and safety in the angels"; it emerged from that driven inclination toward perfection, and from the vision of a goal through which he would become at the same time creator and creation.

In the notes from his youth Rilke conceived of all art as that thing for which objects wait, in order to be completed and made more truthful and more real than they otherwise might be (1898):

> Art is the dark wish of all things. They want to be the images of our secrets, … concealed and revealed at once: — Depth, unknown connections, not even fathomed by the artist. They have become so similar.

Now, to the extent that his corporeality was nailed to his inner experience, that which was artistically apprehended achieved a corporeality beyond all art, and amidst other things radiated in a more than simply earthly light:

> And regardless of the cheerful moons that reflected
> the purest suns of the world, it is perhaps only
> through the backside that is always turned away from
> us that we relate to infinite space.

He wrote those words from his last apartment in Germany (Ainmillerstrasse, Munich in January, 1919), where he had expected to spend another winter together with me.

This attraction to the otherworldly resulted from the discord between his physical and intellectual sides of the self;

each struggled to represent the whole and would not surrender its supremacy. This even affected his appearance. In an unfathomable way, this seemed to be the case and it disturbed me greatly, like an omen of the future. His expression almost lacked aging, the natural aging to which the years are entitled and which not only marks a decline but bears an inscription; but, instead of this, his features ceased to be totally his own. His eyes stood enlarged and afraid, as if they knew that something had happened to his face, as if they asked if an unknown someone could make it right again. Nose, mouth, chin, neck became more strange—even if we were not talking about comprehending something so intangible and even if there were many periods when it completely softened again. That he himself was aware of this odd quality was confirmed in a brief conversation that we had many years ago after a long separation. We were remembering how in the past, when in keeping with the waxing and waning of his moods, he had sometimes appeared winged and other times extinguished, and, so, we had assigned names to these dual appearances: "Rainer" and the "other." When I remarked that I sensed this duality less often than in the past and that I had a stronger impression of an unequivocal response on his part, he looked at me with indescribable sorrow. And nothing could reproduce the look in those large eyes or the tone of his quiet voice, as he responded in a stutter, "Yes, it's clear; I'm right now—the other."

Against the "other" who assumed his own place in earthly matters, there grew a helpless rage: that one could not rid oneself of one's body, that sneering adversary, and still remain a visible functioning being; that creativity gave rise to a peripheral reality, a being of appearances. The suspicion grew that he had perhaps falsely spared himself in the interest of self-preservation:

> But who hasn't been restored and smashed to pieces before.
> And I go around for years like a weakling worrying only that nothing be taken from me.

If only, above all else, the work progressed: this became more and more his first priority — that which was invisible could do what it would with him, he was left to his own devices.

So that this creative energy could be used up and transformed into something that is discovered and felt — into things and animals, whatever, and, if it must, into monsters, he had written only a few years earlier.

In spite of it all, that last German year, our winter together, the spring and early summer in Munich, were still full of hours ripe in hope. In which one knew, sensed: the work, that suffered unborn in him would become something — but what of *him*? What would become of *him*?

There was no thought of resettling in Switzerland. He had only intended to spend a few summer months there. We had set a date in October for a reunion in Germany. We did this in the last moments on the railway platform, before I departed. His wife and a few friends were with us. All was well. But as we chatted and joked and the train began to move slowly, I became deeply concerned and the dark words from one of his Parisian letters weighed heavily on my mind.

… But I go, like the animals—close season is over.

Rilke's alienation from or dissatisfaction with himself as a person stands in some relation to that distinctive eroticism that marked his poetic style during the last decade. Could one characterize it almost as a conscious turning away from the listener, from the reader? We often spoke about this. At first, it appeared to be a most obvious consequence of what he had acquired during the Rodin period: an antipathy toward the "retreat from the object to the observation of the effect," through which artistic endeavor all too often became the most vain of trades. An absolute surrender to accomplishing the work at hand, "steadfastly bending over the tool," without a side-glance to superficial finesse. That is most visually and palpably executed in the *New Poems*, in which there are places in the most beautiful ones where that which is described may be grasped by the senses as if modeled by hand, and a stanza flows like an outpouring of the spirit that can no longer retain its internal relation and reference; it cannot be sustained by the real reproduction. As soon as Rilke's subject matter was derived more and more from the interior of the object and not from that which was externally palpable, it was transformed slowly into oaths that barely allowed for participation. The acquired power that expression exercises on reality celebrates its triumph here, but in actuality it is audible only to those who are capable of experiences of the same expectant magnitude and unresolved depth. To others the poet can sometimes appear to be a Moses who, coming down from the mountain, is totally preoccupied by his revelation and neglects to write out fully the ten commandments. In fact, this unintentional penchant for the esoteric was not seldom mistaken for an intentional mannerism. But here it was so fully the poet himself who "wrestled with God" that the dislocated hip became for him an honor; and only those whose lives are similarly endangered by such a struggle find in him truly their poet.

In the years before the time in Switzerland — where he translated piece by piece the Michelangelo sonnets and perfected some beautiful poems — as later, following 1922 and the *Duino Elegies*, Rilke became preoccupied with translations. That does not mean that he was filling time with semi-productive pursuits, but rather that he devoted himself as fully to this as he did to his own work. But surely such a form of work may have served as a refuge from the afflictions of his spirit, so that it calmed him and protected him for the moment (similar to the "trap" in which one is both exposed and withdrawn). One must also take into account that the object of a translation closely approximates Rodin's notion of material, that which is objectified and carried across but which one cannot exact sufficiently to do justice to it. As such, there is a compromise implicit in the work, between the exact manufacture of the exterior of the work and the extraordinary internalization, that conjures up "material" from the farthest reaches and depths for the work itself. Aside from all this, translations hold an especially strong appeal for such a mystical empathizer as Rilke. Even during the earliest days of our friendship, with only a rudimentary knowledge of French, Rilke did not refrain from translating French as well as writing original verse in that language. It is perhaps more noteworthy that on the long journey through Russia he did the same in Russian: out of deep longing, verse —although grammatically suspect—inexplicably poetic emerged. (The poems' titles mark the order of their birth: "First Song," "Second Song," "Morning," "Old Man," "Passion," "Countenance.") Nothing would be more incorrect than to ascribe Rilke's preoccupation with foreign languages to an antipathy toward his homeland—as was falsely done during the last year of his life when he published his own poems written in French; the opposite is true. Once during an extended stay of several years in Paris, when I voiced the fear that his absence might ultimately alienate him from a crucial intimacy with German, he responded in animated fashion: "Oh no! This intimacy actually thrives on it (alienation). Consider only how many words I save through not using them up on the banalities of daily life." Before he translated Paul Valéry, he had tried his hand at French verse. He felt himself bound not only as an artist to Valéry— there was something that reminded him of the long, almost silent times that preceded the *Elegies* and could not possibly follow them. He writes from Château de Muzot:

> You know that he, P.V.—after several early publications—was almost completely silent for twenty-five

years, concerned with mathematics, and only since 1919 has he lived again in poetry; and now each line to its very cadence is marked by a deep sense of repose to which no one of us has access. How magnificent.

During his stay in Switzerland, Rilke went for a brief time to Paris; he stayed there only for six days, without seeing anyone, but it constituted for him a liberating reunion with unforgettable impressions from the past (although he had his fill of Paris even before 1914, and only with much effort in the fall of 1913 could I talk him into returning there). Just after his return from Paris (1920), his Swiss friends gave him a fortuitous gift; they provided him with a castle, Schloss Bergam Irchel, in the canton of Zurich:

> This little old castle Berg—mine, for me quite alone, like the wintry solitude. Berg, far from any access by train, is difficult to reach, more so because of the quarantine imposed on account of lockjaw and hoof-and-mouth disease, it is even more remote. Consequently, I have not been able to leave the boundaries of the park for weeks—but each limitation of this kind only reinforces my protection and safety.

For the duration, the fountain in the park remained "his only companion." The same loneliness surrounds him in his later home, in the Château de Muzot above Sierre (Valais). For, in contrast to earlier times, home represented something quite different for him; it did not mean as it once had "stepping under one roof." Home was neither a protective shield from a reality not yet experienced, nor was it a haven from work where one's energies were replenished. Now he only sought protective walls to surround the expected event—that which was solely important and real. As he wrote on September 10, 1921, it was originally meant to be only a living experiment:

> I fear this is too hard for me. To live within it is like standing in a heavy rusty armor. And one looks out through the slits of the helmet onto a beckoning heroic land.

Also, the climate with its superabundance of beloved light seemed to pose a too difficult challenge. As time progressed, he felt this more and more:

The sun here works exclusively for the wine; wine is her métier. She oppresses everything else—plants, animals, and human beings—and burdens them with the weight of her hatching which is exactly timed for the vineyards. (Muzot, after Easter, 1924)

Still he remained happy about his enduring confinement:

> It turns out that I sit in my strong little tower;—Wish me nothing more than good health and that it is long and uninterrupted.

First of all, post-war conditions—the forced Czech nationalization—stood in the way of his return to Germany. Later he was not even able to attend his daughter Ruth's wedding. He also never saw his little grandchild, the "little virtuous Christine." His second granddaughter, Josepha, was born two months after his death.

And this loneliness full of expectation allowed for less and less written correspondence:

> It seems as if it can only be verbally achieved. More and more than previously every communication has become a challenge to communicate orally, and it will become increasingly the case, the more that one thing is intended (meant, and as such, be it directed internally or externally, it reproduces one and the same thing).

It also troubled him that he no longer dared to do things —that he kept too much to himself:

> A few days ago, someone offered me a dog. You can imagine what a temptation that was, especially since the remote location of this house makes the presence of a protector almost advisable. But I felt that engaging such a housemate would result in too great a commitment. Everything and everyone who makes claims on me forces me to treat them justly and in the end I retreat when I sense that they might consume me fully.

In Wolfratshausen around 1897 and years later in Rome, he had similar experiences with a dog. Then he feared that he was completely unable to care for a trusting animal that required so little attention. Now he feared that such a limited association would sap him of all his energies. Still, it seemed that a personal tone could be heard in his letters, as if it came from a distinctly personal need or from a peculiar nostalgia for home. In the same letter he writes:

> And think that my study and the adjacent small bedroom in this suite remind me especially at evening (in ways that are not easily described) of the upper rooms in Waldfrieden in Schmargendorf—a breed of small "ladybugs" is spending the winter with me (that too could also happen in Schmargendorf)....
>
> December 29, 1921

Waiting and persisting, he sat there, eyes closed to the fearful menace of what was never completed, hands flatly placed on his knees. He was surrounded by the grand order of a completely regulated daily regimen, for this made him feel safe and prepared. Order seemed to come naturally to him. Much like his occasional pedantry, it always represented a corrective instinct against the effects of poetic rapture. Apart from the extremes of character that played off of each other as reactive imbalances, order was something very close to the poet, that held him ready for any departure. He explained as follows:

> Apparently this ordering principle that is one of the most irrepressible of the artist's strengths is evoked by two internal conditions: the consciousness of a superabundance and the complete surrender to its particular demands. This too results in a further surplus.

Year in and year out, and then it occurs in a single day of penetrating insight. In February of 1922 the fragments of the

Elegies—together with the *Sonnets to Orpheus*—were brilliantly cast in the fire, and the great bell assumed its form, hardened, and resounded. He stood there as if in a storm. Like cries in the wind, his words announced the event:

> Lou, dear Lou, this Saturday, on the 11th of February around six o'clock, I lay aside my pen, having completed the last elegy, the tenth—Just think! I have survived to this point.
>
> What a miracle. Everything in a few days. It was a hurricane.
>
> Everything in me that was fiber, texture and framework has cracked and bent.—
>
> And imagine one other thing in another context— I wrote, created the horse. You know, the free happy gray horse with the wooden peg in his foot that once toward evening came upon us in a gallop on the Volga meadow—What is time? When is the present?
>
> He leapt over so many years into the wide open spaces of feeling.—Now? I know myself again. It was really like a mutilation of the heart that the elegies were not there. And now they are. They are.
>
> I went out and stroked little Muzot that has protected me and ultimately preserved me so long, as if it were a great old animal.

And then more cautiously on Sunday:

> Now, just think, in the brilliant aftermath of the storm, yet another elegy has just arrived, that of the

Saltimbanques. It so wonderfully complements the rest. Now, for the first time, the cycle of elegies seems complete. This will not be added as the eleventh but rather incorporated as the fifth, before the "Hero's-Elegy." The piece now standing in its place, although a beautiful poem, seemed to me not right, given its different construction. So the other one will replace this one (and how!) and now this one will come under the rubric "Fragments." The second part of the book of elegies will contain all that was conceived concurrently during that period either devastated before its creation or cut into pieces during its development, and for which there remain only surfaces of fragments. That's what the *Saltimbanques* are.

Yes, I was attracted to them from the earliest days in Paris and I had since then given up on them.

But not enough. This elegy was barely on paper when the *Sonnets to Orpheus* proceeded. Today I am arranging this new group (the second part of them) and I have copies for you, some that I consider the best—

All stemming from this time and still very fresh. Only our Russian horse (Oh, how he greets you, Lou!) is from the earlier first part, from the beginning of the month.

Your old Rainer
The *Elegies* 5, 7 & 9—soon!

The relapse into heightened anxiety could not be avoided. He wrote sadly:

> I know well that there can be a "reaction," — the sense of crashing somewhere, after being hurled so forcefully. But I finally am falling into the approaching spring and then: since I have been patient for so long in order to achieve what is finally accomplished, one would think that I could have a little extra patience for the bad days.
>
> And in the end the gratitude (which I have never had more of) even for them must outweigh the depression and confusion.

In the ensuing couple of years this gratitude fought back and increased so much that it overwhelmed him. On the last day of October in 1925 he spoke of this:

> You wrote me then, when the elegies were just conceived and were there, saved, — that I should not be terrified if one day I experience a relapse and I know that I responded bravely. But now I am terrified, you see, and I live in the middle of my terror.

In 1923 he went to the Sanatorium Valmont, above Montreux, to seek help from Dr. Haemmerli. Toward the end of 1924 he was there again and, because his doctor had recommended a total change of impressions, air and surroundings, he went to Paris on January 8, 1925: into the circle of his new-found friends where he felt himself completely accepted and sufficiently busy.

> But neither did the victory come nor the release. Just imagine that the obsession — was stronger, more powerful than Paris. It became the suffering of a long defeat and if I, quite removed from my protective surroundings, remained in Paris until August, it was only out of shame in returning like the same old afflicted person to my tower.

And from then on, he was visited by more and more precise and acute fears of bodily illnesses, of ulcers, poisonous, internal processes, as if haunted by an encroaching fear of death. It did not let go of him. It pursued him and permeated every mood.

There is no doubt that the relapse from the ecstatic breakthrough of the *Elegies* did not only reflect the ups and downs of the creative process. To the extent that the angels of the *Elegies*, beyond their existence as an aesthetic creation, were more real and marked by an immediacy and presence that overshadowed their creator, his own being was called into question through them. What that hour of inspiration did not immediately embrace, what remained behind, became nothing to the angels, and was destroyed. Beauty, as that which evokes the image of the almighty, is here a reflection, a hallowed light, beyond which a humanly intangible passion flames. And anything that comes a hairbreadth closer to the shining apparition is consumed by the flames and flickers out to nothing:

> For beauty is nothing but the onset
> of terror, that is still bearable,
> and it amazes us, because
> it coolly deigns to destroy us.

"First Elegy"

The essential point here is that what in art is touched by beauty exists of itself, apart from the mediator of its expression. It is the point where art and belief, creation and prayer, converge. Belief, indeed credibility, appear here to be the last step that art in its most extreme ecstasy undertakes toward its outermost boundaries—thereby extending beyond itself and its hallowed appearance into the destructive flames of passion. This did not necessarily have to pose a threat to all that was human and not art, had Rilke in accustomed style been a "pious believer" in the sense of some form of faith (irrespective of its dogmatic or speculative direction). Its soul-saving, healing effects would have embraced him as well, for it contains an emergency support: as both its primary purpose and its reason. Nothing lay further from his perspective. He stood erect before that which belief offers—not in the posture of the petitioner but rather as one who responds to his duty, not passively, but driven by his own artistic urge, that same artistry that had left him seeming so hopelessly impotent and vulnerable with respect to practical life. Never pausing in his care for the work, never considering the sacrifice implicit in his poetic proclamation,

the human concern, that insight into that greater presence
might kill him.

> That someday at the end of this terrifying vision,
> I might sing praise and jubilation to the assenting
>   angels,
> that the heart's clear striking hammers not fail
> to fall on soft, doubting or torn strings.
> that my streaming countenance make me more
>   radiant;
> that this unseemly crying bloom —

Thus begins the "Tenth Elegy," fragments of which belong to the earliest outpourings. He stood upright, without
complaint, steadfast in his own particular manliness.

For the angels are not intermediaries, and that is important. For him there were no mediating saints or redeemers,
although the name of the angels may have come from his
Catholic childhood. For him God remained for all time the
designation for the all-embracing unity. If in *The Book of
Hours* God is addressed only as a "neighbor," it is because
the slightest removal from him would pose an absolute and
hopelessly insurmountable distance. What is presented here,
instead, before the dominion of the heavens over the earth, is
the horizon of angels, an optically unifying illusion. When
perceived at a distance, the impression produces a blinding
vertigo. The extreme intimacy of the appeal — perhaps, one
might say, so familiar as to make it "useless" — has become

here unnameable, as if its very articulation might overempha-
size the angels' rapture, the beating of their wings.

And yet it correctly reads:

> … oh pain.
> that I still sing to you …
> knowing who you are …
> … Who are you?
> Early blessed ones, creation's spoiled darlings,
> Peaks, ranges, morning-red ridges,
> of all creation, — pollen of a blossoming divinity,
> joints of light, hallways, steps, thrones,
> spaces of essence, shields of ecstasy, tumultuous
> storms of excited feeling and suddenly, separate,
> mirrors, restoring their once drained beauty
> back again into their own faces.

"Second Elegy"

They are what we could only dream to be and in this way
we are damned. Their real existence prevents us from also
losing our essence. Only in denial and doubt we ask desper-
ately:

> Does the cosmic space
> into which we dissolve taste of us at all? Do the
>   angels really
> only absorb their own effusions
> or is there sometimes, as if by mistake,
> a little of our being there too? Are we mixed

into their features as slightly as the vague look
on a pregnant woman's face? They do not notice it in
   the swirling
return to themselves. (How could they notice it?)
"Second Elegy"

In juxtaposition to their reality, what allows us to cease being is precisely our physical being, that which cannot escape into such a reality, the greatest limitation over and against such ambition, material being. As it always had been from the beginning, in Rilke's struggle the body bore the suffering. In his youth he had feared the body as the inescapable point of contact between the pressing threat of the external world and the secure longing of his interior being. As such, he had regarded the body with mistrust and suspicion, as the source of his own undoing. It made him feel "a little guilty," as he had once remarked in a written self-portrait. And now it had become indelibly marked with the horrifying distinction of separateness from the realm of the angels. Blameless, if you will, but predestined to a kind of humiliating hard labor, given over to the counter-angelic confusion and tumult of grotesque imitation.

> It is a vicious cycle, a circle of black magic that encloses me as if in a Breughel painting of hell. My true nature is now buried in the duration and madness of the search for home and this overwhelming fear suffices to estrange me from myself. I don't see how I can live this way any longer—

The expression "true nature" (in another instance at the conclusion, "growing nature") refers to the actual innocence and naivete of the body left to its own devices and abandoned by the realm of the angels. And this circumscribes the hellishness of the situation. For a feeling of guilt would include a rueful, suspicious sense of humanity surrendered to the damned—and would lead to discord and the questioning of where one indeed belongs. In contrast, this is precisely the reason that "hell" cannot admit of redemption, because it ambiguously captivates and binds us: also in the sense of an incomprehensible, secret attraction. From thence emerges the counterpart of God; that is, the God who is turning away again, the "deus inversus" in *his* kingdom—the gap, as it were, in the omnipresence of God, to employ the extreme language of Christian dogma. That his hell could appear this way is closely related to the perfection of the angels' spiritual nature and the extreme power that their reality wields, according to the law that the summit first reveals the abyss and the light casts its truth in the shadows.

The otherworldliness of the proclamation of the angels' existence, the progressive divestiture of reality, the debasement of the earthly, is not the sole character of the *Elegies*. In them the earthly achieved its expression with the ardor of an incessant avowal of self, as barely witnessed before. Not merely in indulgence as in *The Book of Hours* in which the poet confronts in each and every thing his God—the poet who creates on the spot and has created all poetry in the real thing—but something quite different: in man's struggle to interest these strange beings, the angels, in his earth. In this way, all that is earthly is suspended without artistic flaw in the *Elegies*: a little like a child who displays his self-made toys to the wealthier and propertied adults, in modest gestures yet with passionately proud candor:

> Praise the world to the angel, not the unsayable,
> you can't impress him with grand emotion;
> in the cosmos,
> where he feels so much more, you are a novice.
> So show
> him some simple thing, shaped from generation to
> generation,
> that lives and belongs to us, in our hands and in
> our gaze.
> Tell him of things. He will stand more amazed, just as
> you did
> beside the ropemaker in Rome or the potter on
> the Nile.

"Ninth Elegy"

Such lapidary sentences stand there: enhanced by the memories of the Rodin period, of the sufficiency of the most lifeless, loveless material, that in human hands appeared sacrosanct to the observing gaze of man, like a glass on the dinner table. And much more: memories of everything filled with life and spirit belonging to us, like the intimate things from the divine childhood of *The Book of Hours*. The passion of those memories overflows: should it not be the most private and native things of the earth that suspend their palpability and are delivered into the realm of the invisible as our most cherished enduring property?:

> Earth, isn't this what you want: invisibly
> to resurrect in us? …
> What, if not transformation, is your urgent mission?
> Earth, beloved, I will!

"Ninth Elegy"

A hope stands there trembling: a love of the earth and creation to the last speck of dust on the pathway as toward a love, imbued with a heart that can never enter the realm of the angels, that can never fear for itself alone, because it can conceive of itself only as a totality. But the power of this ardor does not touch the angels, those "almost dead birds of the soul." For every angel is terrifying. And trembling the cry breaks forth, in spite of the struggle to repress without complaint "the call-note of sobbing":

> Who, if I cried out, would hear me in the ranks of
> angels? And were one suddenly to take me
> to his heart, I would dissipate in his stronger presence.

"First Elegy"

If one asks how the stronger presence allows that which is human not only to perish but to enter into the anxieties of damnation, one touches upon the third principle of the *Elegies*, beyond those governing the angelic and earthly orders. The earthly order embraces individual experience that is transferred to generations, in the endlessness of sequential forms, deeply rooted in a primal existence. In total innocence the individual approaches:

> his inner wilderness,
> the primeval forest, where his pale green heart
> stood among the mute ruins ...
> Loving he descended into the older blood, into the
>   canyons
> where terror lay, still gorged by his fathers.
> And every horror knew him and winked in collusion.
> Yes, atrocity smiled at him ...

"Third Elegy"

As such, physical being is the final word for terror; out of the blood that has for time and eternity circulated within us, atrocity laughs devilishly, no longer threatening but in the cheerful and ironic dance of victory. Projection into the mystical juxtaposition to the angels, into that horrible revenge for the powerful consistency, corporeality, and presence which the angels beyond artistic creation have absorbed for themselves into their being. There is something about this, that destroys individual experience, even apart from its abysmal depths, and severs it from a sense of origin and allows it to sink into groundlessness — that sublimates what is seen to mere appearance, to deception. Here and there, since the inception of the *Elegies*, a similar fear was awakened in him. He expressed it repeatedly (as in a letter from Paris dated June 8, 1914) that he sometimes caught sight of himself:

...as if in a museum display case. The glass reflects and I see nothing but my face, the old, earlier, previous one that you know so well.

Then past and future seem to converge into one thin line, leaving no width for the present—a ghostly line that refused to admit that something could happen or had happened. Then fear would grip Rilke's heart, exactly like the fear that had pursued him from postwar Venice, because there amidst the denial of all that had transpired in the interim, the prewar experience seemed to return and haunt him scornfully.

He always remained conscious of the fact that his only defense against this lay in the total immersion in his most forgotten memories, in those that directly touched the moment when the individual in his particular experience is separated from his primal origins. Are not these the ones that arise ghost-like in the creative hours? To the poet of the *Elegies* they seemed to be blessings, as if granted to only the most favored. But he, the man, derived no final pleasure from that hour of ecstasy and its legacy, the work. The human impulse in creativity was so strong that the created work seemed to overpower him like an intense horrible reality that expelled from itself the human element as insufficient residue. It no longer grounded him in the primal roots of his own past experience, as the prerequisite for the evolving work. But rather precisely there where he wished to find his footing, he was left feeling more groundless than ever.

As is the case for a pregnant woman, work and reality,

the soul's rapture and corporeality were to become for Rilke one and the same. A unity, imparted to him in that which was born, blessedly granted to him and experienced in every fiber of his being. When that was not the case, he encountered the impossible, and no heroic effort that he summoned up, no victim that he conjured could save him; he would be extinguished instantly as a sacrificial victim and become a mere obstacle to the monstrous unity of being that he so ardently sought to grasp. Here ruination touches deeply and gently a dark rapture, in his death before the heart of the "stronger presence." This sinister possibility eludes awareness, because it is experienced entirely as anxiety and torment, and yet it affects the frightful denial of the body, the exposed protective shell, that has only to be dismantled, to demolish his prison and to open up his basically deceitful and bewildering trap-door. Who does not recall the childhood experience when little Rainer struggled before the standing mirror to extricate himself from his masquerade, until, choked with fear, he lay writhing near death on the floor? Between those two moments lies a life. The fear of being destroyed by terrible illness that plagued him in his later years was in fact as much the fear of being in his own body, fastened with clamp-irons in something that forces one to be what one is not. Release from everything, like the fall into damnation, yes—the final awaited fall into the eternal womb. And he, no longer the pregnant one, but left only with what he had so singularly desired to achieve—an eternally secure childhood.

Rainer Maria Rilke died on December 29, 1926 with symptoms of a chronic sepsis[9] A history of monitoring his health and years spent in a favorable climate gave no indication of threatening leukemia. In words weakly penned from his deathbed, he thanked his friends and those who attended him during his illness.

That was what he was still humanly capable of experiencing. But far beyond that, the single sentence stands:

"Oh, this infernal region."

The address and farewell were in Russian.

The re-creation of Rilke's life and work lends itself to three forms of interpretation: the pursuit of an assessment of his artistic worth; the attempt at a psychological study of his life and work; and, finally, the recollection of personal experiences shared with him. All three possible approaches could yield a wealth of insight, even if one does share Rilke's own doubt about the excavation of the great things of the past (expressed in a letter about Rome's monuments):

> … our admiration of them does them a distinct injustice, especially if we recognize a definite and describable beauty in them, for they have buried their faces in the earth and renounce all appellation and meaning. And when man discovered them, they raised themselves effortlessly above the earth and almost lost themselves among the birds. They are so much the essence of space that they preside like stars over inconstant time.

What is sketched here consciously discredits the three above-mentioned approaches: be it the critique of his art, the psychological study, or the assessment of biographical data. If one is to infer from a single correspondence a reply, it becomes almost an act of repeated appropriation of that which has vanished, the last reunion — dialogue. One could almost ask: why turn to others?

The question arises because there is a point nevertheless where Rainer Maria Rilke's life and death extended beyond him and achieved a relevance to everything, and this was exemplified in the meaningful relation of his life to his death. Because it was concerned not merely with the typical moments of surge and decline within creativity; nor did it have to do with the atypical martyrdom of that exclusive relation between individual creative talent and pathology. One thing emerges from such general and specific processes that bears emphasis: the deadly fate of one who as an artist forges ahead to the extreme, to his destination beyond art, where he finds himself no longer accepted. On this outermost boundary, where he succeeded in articulating the unsayable, he paid for this paradise with a descent into the realm of the sayable, the domicile of man. At such junctures, works arise that are permeated with that which was barely suspected, as if those things were tangible realities that could not be contrived through mere genius alone. The songs of his brother, the German poet Friedrich Hölderlin, including the very last ones, emerge from the same origin. But they emanate from the other side, for in the case of that writer of hymns, the mental illness that enveloped him and broke through the bounds relieved the conscious human being from the poetic consequences of his fantasy and led him to destruction. Were one to imagine that the mentally healthy Rilke, a stalwart fighter for harmony, had accomplished just that ideal, then two possibilities present themselves: first, that he accomplished what was most possible for him in a direction other than hymnic elegy, and, second, that the redemptive harmony that struggled for perfection within himself was achieved at the expense of the artistic. Indeed, in order to accomplish this, his sharpest thorn was removed in the interest of the production of the work. For from the earliest times, the deepest arousal of his poetic fantasy had remained a human longing for the most corporeal reality. This sliced through all artistic contrivance in a peculiar kind of appropriation of self that actually did violence to him.

One must bear in mind how much all imagination, together with its offspring, art, is nothing more than a mode of expression serving a great power within us, the insufficiency of that which is immediately available. Poetically expressed, it is always the newly formed bridge between that which is sayable and does not always carry the imperative to replenish reality and that which is rational as if all imagination stemmed from a broad knowledge within which logic and practical existence cannot keep pace with each other. Now, instead of functioning merely as a bridge, their offspring, art, can go too far in its attempt to present the far-reaching path itself. It can either damage the work of art through disproportionately burdening it with real life content, or, conversely, it can fail to satisfy human conscious experience through relegating its content to the symbolic references of its forms. On the one hand, the "sayable" dares to want to be more than the palpable image and symbolic expression of our most mute, stilled impressions and it places itself noisily in their stead. On the other hand, we overlook the fact that artistic forms as such already reflect the content of the "unsayable," and we assign autonomy to the external form, to mere artistry. Between tendentiousness and formal artistry, all art stands in danger of being deprived of its sense of mediation, its meaning. But, in each case, however much art's meaning serves its own end, it remains committed to both directions, the tie between both that uniquely restores a unity for us. And precisely for this reason, without any latitude—yes, without even a crack, tear, or sovereign space for itself. If it appears sometimes otherwise, that is, if art overexerts itself to present more than expression, it take vengeance on itself in the way that it takes vengeance on the poet: it acquires a reality by robbing human experience of its inviolable space and hurls it to a deadly fate. The great threshold work is erected and its creator is sacrificed.

One cannot have lingered long at Rilke's grave without realizing with a certain shudder how casually and naively we gloss over the final evidence that is to be found in what we call art. It would almost seem that our ordinary attitude toward art would, at the very least, dispose us to think about just this. As if our common insincerity, long-windedness and ostrich-like attitude toward internal events were here publicly and obviously sanctioned. As if our basic attitude toward art was, without question, concerned with the most harmless things, unrelated to us. Indeed, we place art prominently in the foreground, yes, to an extent, in the center of attention, and we judge man according to the reception and understanding of art. We teach our children to genuflect before her, long before a child's judgment has matured, yet this is of no importance. In so doing, we act as if what really mattered was "genuine, great, pure art," in contradistinction to that which is tendentious and entertaining. We demand education in order to penetrate art's formal laws and comprehend it aesthetically; we angrily deny that a direct, albeit long, line runs from art to other aspects of life, because a clear dividing line should remain between both. Here art, there non-art. But while we talk art into this dangerous position, we assure ourselves that we have nothing to fear from its accidental upsetting effects. For precisely this reason, art becomes something aloof from life, a matter of acquired taste, a property of the privileged classes, a higher form of pleasure beside that of the banal. Our occasional insights into the catastrophic element of creation and its consequences for the creator change nothing of this.

Now, in the meantime, emotional upheavals about that which is acquired or has become conventional may result: firsthand experience of the work of art that can have a powerful influence on the child. But exactly here, where an inner adjustment in our attitude toward art might take place, a fundamental perversion is revealed. For in order for that to occur, art must lay claim to life and not assume an ancillary role and fear the organic union with the internal intention of things; we must admit that this emanates from the most human primitive stirrings toward the perfection of the work of art and that it serves this basic unity, indeed makes it possible. If this is not true, then it is questionable whether the deeper effect of art on youth and its development is even desirable; for then it saps youth of the strength that life requires and expends it peripherally. Then art is a suggestion that diverts and weakens—a tempting, harmful preoccupation to which words like "depravity" and "debauchery" could be applied. That this strikes us as strange, senseless and unfeeling, and that this moralistically places us in the wrong, shows how much we live in the uncertainty of our own instincts, how little informed we are of our own life.

To be sure, there is another attitude toward art that is not taken into account here. One finds it behind all art and complicated expressive forms of imagination. One finds it in the mere fact that every one of us leads an imaginative existence, from the most primitive to the most sophisticated levels of our experience, from our most waking thoughts to our deepest nightly dreams. And the more removed we are from controlling consciousness, the more immersed we become in the wellsprings of psychic darkness: the more convinced we become of the poet who resides within us and within everyone. He certainly does not allow himself to be expelled from the focal point of his effect. He stoops even more darkly when he is approached in order to hide himself more effectively in the seclusion of his work. Between the consciousness that we rightfully cultivate within ourselves and the realm of unconscious organisms, the poet does not allow his bridges to crumble; although, when we cannot spare the time to acknowledge them, we amble for ever and ever on their pathways. And this part of man's creative potential belongs not merely to the internal estate of the healthy common man; it reaches down into the most humiliating strata, where emotional fragility and neediness threaten to drive us to distraction, ensnare us in misguided impulses, from which only the most conscious elucidation of perspective can deliver us. Precisely in such states, it can happen that, as a result of having been drawn into an abyss, we near those deep pathways upon which the artist erects his work into consciousness. As if, in pursuing internally the core of man, the poet crosses the same path, upon which the psychically ill patient gropes aimlessly before him. The healthy person cannot fathom through rational means what ominously sways back and forth between the two on such occasions. But I would personally call upon the experience of Rilke to attest to the fact that such an experience could also be relished by the creative person, indeed be a greater source of encouragement than any form of critical applause from connoisseurs or fellow poets. Perhaps in this way he recalled the old longing to become a doctor, a healer, and helper, as if only in so doing could help for himself be guaranteed. After I told him of a patient who, completely uneducated in art, for the first time derived hope from the *Elegies* — a recognition of their indescribably illuminating power and their hopeful access to order and peace—a response came from the Château de Muzot on the Tuesday just after Easter in 1924:

> My dear, dear Lou, I can not tell you what a high and mighty Easter your letter has made for me ... ,— First, after I tell you the story of my past (third) Muzot winter, you will understand how wonderful it is that you have reported this about X: I read it over and over again and gleaned from it an indescribable sense of security.

"Security" indicates here that he is first able to achieve it by an indirect route, through those to whom he has given it. Here there is no directed interest in the other, as expressed, for instance, in compassion, humility, ambition, or condescension. There is nothing more to this than the jubilation of that hour in which he wrote of the *Elegies*: "They are, they are!" There can be no stronger proof of their existence for him, who felt himself annihilated in their creation, who consequently suffered extreme self-doubts, and who had to equate them with the success of being, than that destroyed individuals find themselves restored to life through them. By this means, he himself ascends from the crucifixion on Easter, a day that for once, now has meaning for him too: "Today you will be with me in Paradise."

The same circumstance brings him closer to man, standing as an equal on the same ground where we descend into our primal origins—a ground to which the exalted ones have no greater claim than the most humble and toiling aspirants.

I would like to believe that herein lies Rilke's lifelong and compelling need: to prove himself through daily labor, through constant trust in the most humble of things, through respectful attention to the poor and unblessed hours of existence itself. This did not mean that he should function as an apprentice during the lacunae of craftsmanship. But rather that he derive life from that which embraces the most humble as well as the most exalted things, and which consequently render us "safe." And he should accomplish that, despite human consciousness: in the acknowledgment of differences that so urgently and seductively tear us apart in highs and lows, triumphs and failures, heaven and hell, life and death.

Abandoning himself in everything, and thereby making himself superfluous, the benefactor becomes at once the petitioner, the recipients become donors, and he hides in their secure existence. And were this loner, who was isolated in death, still with us, I believe he would feel most immediately at home in the deepest anonymity of his work's effects—there in the no longer audible processes of man's union with the cosmos, where his form is allowed to fade and no longer requires visibility or the boundaries of self. Restored to a stronger presence: standing there, in deep peace, he too a nameless one among the nameless.

Translating a Life:
An Afterword

Rose, oh pure contradiction, joy
To be nobody's sleep under so many
Eyelids.

EPIGRAPH ON RILKE'S GRAVESTONE

In her memoir of Rainer Maria Rilke, Lou Andreas-Salomé refers to Rilke's preoccupation, both in the years before and after writing the Duino Elegies, with the work of translation. She compares the poet's fascination with translation to the sculptor Rodin's notion of "material," which is "objectified and carried across but which one cannot exact sufficiently to do justice to it." (p. 99) And she draws our attention to the implicit compromise of this work, "between the exact manufacture of the exterior of the work and the extraordinary internalization that conjures up 'material' from the farthest reaches and depths of the work itself." (p. 99) There is indeed something in the experience of translation that entails just such a process of bringing depths to a surface that one cannot make claim to, as one's own. This "alien surface" recalls somewhat Lou's characterization of Rilke's stance toward his own body—that precarious stage where the external and the internal are thrust together and agree to appear as one and the same. The body, if you will, as translator of the soul.

For the translator, the work of carrying over or re-creating a life suggests an embodiment of voice that, however closely rendered, must ultimately be disowned. And that is the work of Lou's memoir in creating an intimate portrait of

Rilke with barely a trace of the artist—that is, herself—and no audible self-referential note that might separate her from the object. In some sense, she is enacting Rilke's own lived belief that all true art requires a final surrender of the artist to the object.

Certainly in preparing this translation (and as-yet-unpublished translations of much of Rilke and Lou Andreas-Salomé's correspondence), I too have found myself enticed by the thrills and danger of ventriloquizing their voices. I have for once grasped Rilke's personal frustration and insight into the greater compatibility of imagery with the graphic arts, precisely because the graphic arts render tangible results. By contrast, poetry issues from an internal landscape —a realm of intangible causes. Indeed, in such a saturated age of imagery as our own, words are all the proof we have of the soul and yet they are the elusive object of the art itself. They are inspiration to the poet and the tools for the translator. They expose interiors—inner material—that cannot be replicated and hence represent a formidable, perhaps even insurmountable challenge to any translator.

To read the correspondence between these passionate friends is to become deeply aware of Lou's active role as Rilke's translator of his life. As such, the memoir itself is the culminating event and natural extension of that lifetime service. On numerous occasions, well past their early love affair, Rilke wrote to Lou appealing not only for comfort but illumination of life's confusions. His open plea to be the focal point of Lou's affections and attention becomes almost an expected refrain in their correspondence. An early letter (August 1, 1903) from Rilke to Lou speaks to just that function as interpreter of his life's events:

> … I am so happy that especially since my writing is so unsteady and fragmentary, I can now at least give you the two books, from which you will be able to recognize my growth. And, Lou, do not let yourself tire of my trifling letters. It means so much to me that I am able to tell you of everyday events, which present me with so much confusion because I have no perspective on them. Before you they become ordered and another thing. And that I know this, helps me more than I can say.
>
> Aug. 1, 1903

Several years later, made weary by the toils of his art and plagued by illness, Rilke characterizes his constant refuge in Lou's presence as a cyclical return to origins through which he can measure his progress:

> … Goodbye, dear Lou; God knows, your presence was so truly the door through which I first came into the open; now I always return from time to time and place myself against the door-post on which we used to mark my growth, long ago. Allow me this fond habit and like me anyway. — Rainer
>
> December 28. 1911

An afterthought to a letter written from the isolation of Château de Muzot underscores the significance of Lou's limitless guardianship as Rilke wrestles to create and tame his angel:

> Dear Lou, somehow you have helped me infinitely, the rest is now for me and the angel, if we only hold fast to each other: he and I, and you from afar.
>
> Oct. 21, 1913

And as testimony to Lou's role as gatekeeper of his poetic soul, Rilke writes nearly a decade later from Château de Muzot to announce the existence of the long-awaited elegies and to entrust them into her keeping:

> Lou, dear Lou, look now: At this moment, this Saturday, the eleventh of February, at six o'clock, I lay aside my pen, having completed the last Elegy, the tenth. The one (even then it was destined to become the last), the beginning of which was already written in Duino: *Dass ich dereinst am Ausgang der grimmigen Einsicht / Jubel und Ruhm aufsinge zu-stimmenden Engeln ...* So much as there was I read to you, but only the first twelve lines have remained, all the rest is new and: yes, very very very magnificent! Just think! —I have survived to this point. Through everything. Miracle, Grace.—Everything in a few days. It was a hurricane, as at Duino back then: all that was fiber, texture, framework, cracked and bent ... Now I know myself again. It was really like a mutilation of my heart that the Elegies were not there....
>
> Feb. 11, 1922

The following year Rilke would inscribe a first edition copy of the *Duino Elegies* with these words of endearment: "For Lou / who has from the beginning / possessed with me / what is finally formed here." He continued throughout the remainder of his life to send poems and fragments to Lou and repeatedly expressed his joy that they were in her hands, "living with" Lou. The final appeal would come from Frau Wunderly-Volkart, Rilke's deathbed attendant, whom he had instructed to divulge the details of his illness only to Lou in the hope of some final saving grace or postmortem insight into his life. So, in the end, when faced with the choice of writing about her great lost friend or speaking in his stead, Lou chose the latter and in her memoir translated Rilke's muted voice from the silence. Her memoir would celebrate the moment when, freed from his body, the poet becomes his art.

Lou's stance is consonant with the invocation of Rilke's spirit that forms the opening lines of the memoir. Lou is herself listening to the stirrings. The cacophonic polarities and contradictory attraction between art and love and art and community (which we saw in the transformed meaning that both Worpswede as well as Russia came to have for Rilke)— those tensions that plagued the poet in his lifetime—merge here at last into the delta of Lou's words, a memoir of such exquisite thoughtfulness and passion that one feels it a final response to a lifetime of accumulated entreaties. And, for a brief time, the suffering doubts of the possibility of ever knowing oneself through the other are suspended, as here in the memoir we find this deserving poet as we do in his poems—"restored to a stronger presence." (p. 127)

Translation, whether it be of life or of poetry itself, whether it be pony or Pegasus, relies on the strength of metaphor to transport us unbound by time or space between the world to which we are born and inhabit and the one that is being created. Indeed, in an essay on translating Shakespeare, the Russian poet Boris Pasternak spoke to this very transcendental function of metaphorical language in negotiating the passage from life to death. "Metaphorical language is the result of the disproportion between man's short life and the immense and long-term tasks he sets himself. Because of this he needs to look at things sharply as an eagle and to convey his visions in flashes that can be immediately apprehended. This is just what poetry is. Outsize personalities use metaphor as a shorthand of the spirit." (Pasternak, *I Remember: Sketch for an Autobiography* [Cambridge: Harvard University Press, 1983] p. 126) Consider the brevity of Rilke's lifetime, then the immensity of a poetic legacy that has survived many generations. If Lou's memoir does anything at all to connect the moment of Rilke's life with the enduring spirit of his art, it is not to translate Rilke's art into his life but quite conversely and consciously, it is to translate his life into art. Such a translation of the man through his art was, after all, the only mode through which Lou had been able to embrace Rilke fully in life and now bade him farewell in death.

At the end of her memoir Lou invokes this destiny for the poet she recalls to her imagination, writing that, were he still with us, he would feel most at home in the anonymity of his works' effects. Anonymous among the nameless. Such beauty as we know to haunt Rilke's poetry seems almost incompatible with the utter humility of such a destiny. Lou's words might seem disingenuous if they had not profoundly echoed the sentiment expressed by the poet several years earlier in famous lines on the integration of art and death from the thirteenth poem of the second cycle of the *Sonnets to Orpheus*:

> Sei allem Abscheid voran, als wäre er hinter
> dir, wie der Winter, der eben geht.
> Denn unter Wintern, ist einer so endlos Winter,
> dass, überwinternd, dein Herz überhaupt übersteht.
>
> Sei immer tot in Eurydike—singender steige,
> preisender steige zurück in den reinen Bezug.
> Hier, unter Schwindenden, sei, im Reiche der Neige,
> sei eine klingendes Glas, das sich im Klang
>   schon zerschlug.
>
> Sei—und wisse zugleich des Nicht-Seins Bedingung,
> den unendlichen Grund deiner innigen Schwingung,
> dass du sie völlig vollziehst dieses einzige Mal.
>
> Zu dem gebrauchtem sowohl, wie zum dumpfen
>   und stummen
> Vorrat der vollen Natur, den unsäglichen Summen,
> zähle dich jublend hinzu und vernichte die Zahl.

Translation:

Be ahead of all parting, as if it were
behind you, like the winter that just passed by.
For beneath winters, one so endless winter stirs
that only in overcoming winter, can a heart survive.

Be always dead in Eurydice—in fuller voice climb,
in greater praise climb back to a pure relation.
Here amongst the vanishing, be, in the realm of decline,
be a ringing glass that sounds as it is breaking.

Be—and know at once the condition of annihilation
the infinite source of your inner vibration,
That you completely perfect it, just this once.

To both the used-up and consumed, the muffled
    and dumb
reserve of all of nature's grandeur, the unsayable sums,
now add yourself joyfully, too, and cancel the count.

Lou's memoir is thus part of a dialogue of farewells—a counterpoint of winters declared survived—a conversation that wards off the final winter. The last line of Rilke's last letter to Lou, written from his deathbed less than two weeks before his death, warned of an "air of harm in this year's end, something threatening" and the letter was signed atypically in Lou's native Russian: "Farewell, my darling." As if to allay Rilke's menacing fear of the future and to assure him safe passage through the final winter, a year later in this memoir Lou listened to the stirrings and then consigned her charge to the peace and security of the "no longer audible processes of man's union with the cosmos." A remarkable farewell. A memoir of the birth of his poems. A welcoming home of his soul.

REFERENCES

Andreas-Salomé, Lou. *Lebenstrückblick, Grundriss einiger Lebenserinnerungen,* ed. E. Pfeiffer, Zurich and Wiesbaden, 1951. Revised. Frankfurt: Insel, 1977.

Leppmann, Wofgang. *Rilke: A Life.* New York: Fromm International Publishing Corp., 1984.

Livingtone, Angela. *Salomé.* Mount Kisco: Moyer Bell, Ltd., 1984.

Rilke, Rainer M. *Rainer Maria Rilke/Lou Andreas-Salomé: Briefwechsel,* ed. E. Pfeiffer. Frankfurt: Insel, 1975.

Hendry, I. F. *The Sacred Threshold: A Life of Rainer Maria Rilke.* London: Carcanet, 1985.

NOTES

1. Pg 3: *Choice of names*. I have chosen to call Lou by her given name rather than Salomé or Andreas-Salomé, because it was the name she liked most. In her later years, she was known to suggest to new acquaintants that they simply call her "Frau Lou." Salomé seems rigid and Andreas-Salomé cumbersome. I refer to Rainer Maria Rilke as Rilke, the name by which he is best known. So in calling Andreas-Salomé "Lou," I wish not to be overly familiar but to invoke her independent spirit, which is in keeping with the personal voice of her memoir.

2. Pg 21: *Princess Maria Thurn-und-Taxis Hohenloe*. Married to a prince from Bohemia, this member of the Austro-Hungarian Empire was a cultured patron of the arts who cultivated a circle of artists and promoted their work. Twenty years older than Rilke, and a maternal figure, she met the poet in 1909 and carried on a correspondence with him for many years. She lent Rilke her castle Duino on the Adriatic Sea where he wrote the first two elegies, and Rilke later dedicated the entire cycle to her. A learned woman with an

abiding appreciation of Rilke's art, she translated a number of his poems and elegies into Italian. Theirs was a close literary friendship in which she looked after his art and his home life, wrote to his wife Clara and sent gifts to his daughter Ruth, and advised him openly on his friendships. Recognizing his fragile sensibility and his otherworldly nature, she came to call Rilke "Dottor Serafico"—perhaps too a concession to the emerging presence of the "angel" in Rilke's work.

3. Pg. 62 *Ellen Key.* Swedish writer and author of *The Century of the Child*, Key was a lifelong friend of Rilke. Both Lou and Key shared the view of the essential difference between men and women. Key championed the notion that women should first and foremost live for their children, while Lou cited the need for women to discover their innate distinctly female abilities; their insistence on the natural differences of the sexes incited rancor in many feminists of their day.

4. Pg 69: "if only everything were not suspended." In the original letter this line was followed by a direct appeal to see Lou: "If only we could see each other, Lou. That is my greatest wish!"

5. Pg. 71: *Paula Modersohn-Becker.* A painter and friend of Rilke and the sculptor Clara Westhoff who later became Rilke's wife, Modersohn-Becker died in childbirth. Rilke memorialized her in the poem "Requiem for a Woman Friend" (November 1903), in which he juxtaposes the irreconcilable demands of motherhood and art that were

tragically captured in her untimely death just as she was coming into her own as an artist.

6. Pg 71: *Rilke's translations.* Rilke produced a number of texts from the French, including "Love of Magdalen," a sermon by a seventeenth century orator, and "The Portuguese Letters of Marianna Alcorado" in 1911. In 1916 and 1917, when Rilke's poetic output came to a standstill, he sought to break the silence by throwing himself into the work of others. He translated the "Twenty-Four Sonnets of Louise Labe of Lyon"—a sixteenth century poet bemoaning her lot of unrequited love.

7. Pg. 85: *Personal effects seized in Paris.* While visiting Germany, war broke out and Rilke did not return to Paris. His possessions were confiscated and for most of the war, Rilke lived out of a suitcase.

8. Pg. 85: *Rilke's military service.* Rilke was never up to the task of soldiering. Indeed, he was bullied and ridiculed by various drill sergeants. Despite a medical deferment (lung problems), which he did not have a chance to submit to authorities, Rilke ended up serving in the War Archives in Vienna in 1916. He was shortly thereafter released through the efforts of numerous literary figures and his ever-protective Princess Maria Thurn-und-Taxis Hohenloe.

9. Pg 118: *Cause of death.* Rilke died at the age of 51—not of blood poisoning, as was rumored—but of acute leukemia on the morning of December 29, 1926. He never questioned the

doctor about the cause of his sickness, rejected painkillers, and assiduously avoided mention of death until the very end.

10. Pg. 129: *Epigraph*. Despite his aversion to speaking of death, Rilke did pen these lines for inscription on his gravestone:

> Rose, oh reiner Widerspruch, Lust
> Niemandes Schlaf zu sein unter soviel
> Lidern.

His words capture effortlessly the contradiction of the poet's death and his resurrection in his art. It is noteworthy that the German pronunciation of *Lidern* (eyelids) is exactly the same as *Liedern* (songs). Also, the German word for pure (*reiner*) echoes Rilkes's first name Rainer, and is precariously placed next to "contradiction." Hence, Rilke's play with the tensions between literal and musical/metaphorical meanings, as he alludes to the ultimate absence of the poet ("nobody's sleep") and the legacy of so many "songs."

ACKNOWLEDGMENTS

I wish to thank my son, Christopher, for his enduring support and my husband Jim Jordan for his dear encouragement, Stefanie Diaz for her expert preparation of the typescript, and my editor Steven Huff of BOA Editions for his wise and careful editing of the manuscript. Finally, my homage to the spirits of Lou and Rilke for the extraordinary example of their passionate friendship.

—Angela von der Lippe

Из книг Наталии К.

✸

You Alone Are Real to Me: Remembering Rainer Maria Rilke,
was typeset by Valerie Brewster, Port Townsend, Washington,
using Stemple Garamond and Kallos fonts.
The cover was designed by Daphne Poulin-Stofer, Rochester, New York.
Manufacturing was by McNaughton & Gunn, Saline, Michigan.
The publication of this book was made possible, in part, with the
special support of the following individuals:

Nancy & Alan Cameros
Ronald & Susan Dow
Peter & Suzanne Durant
Suressa Forbes
Dr. Henry & Beverly French
Pat Ford
Robert & Adele Gardner
Robert & Rae Gilson
Dane & Judy Gordon
Kip & Deb Hale
Robert & Willy Hursh
Daniel Jacobs
Peter & Phyllis Makuck
Suzanne Owens
Tanya Plutzik
Boo Poulin
Deborah Ronnen
Andrea & Paul Rubery
Annette & Aaron Satloff
Harold Stanley
Jane Schuster
David & Ellen Wallack
Pat & Michael Wilder